MW00944181

MATTER OF TIME

CONTINUE TO MARCH

DAMON ROBERTS SR.

MATTER OF TIME
CONTINUE TO MARCH

iUniverse books may be ordered through booksellers or by contacting:

iUniverse
1663 Liberty Drive
Bloomington, IN 47403
www.iuniverse.com
1-800-Authors (1-800-288-4677)

ISBN: 978-1-5320-8529-1 (sc)
ISBN: 978-1-5320-8530-7 (e)

Library of Congress Control Number: 2019916187

Print information available on the last page.

iUniverse rev. date: 10/17/2019

CONTENTS

ACKNOWLEDGEMENTS

All praises to God/Allah for your grace and mercy in my life!

To my mother BJ, I appreciate your love, guidance, and support throughout my life. This book is deadicated to you

To my wife Maugerite my angel. I appreciate your love, friendship, and support. I enjoy every day with you besides who else can deal with me lol! Luv U!!

To all my children Michelle, Sean, Damon Jr, Danielle, your father loves all of yall very much! Continue to march!!

To all my grandchildren I pray this book inspire you all to achieve whatever your dreams are and the discipline to achieve your goals in live. Luv U!!

To my cousin/sister Dr Juanchella Francis thanks for truly showing me how to study lol! Your life inspires me Chella! Luv U!!

To my cousin/aunt Sandra Brandon your love and daily inspirational scriptures added the rocket fuel to complete this book. Praise God!

To the rest of my family Armetras, Robin, Melody, Jamal, Stacy, Jacki, Sharon, Kim, Tracy, Kelli Jo, and Terri luv yall!!!!

To Ed Hill thanks for modeling what a committed youth coach does in the community for me. "Where your commitment to the kids" lol

To Bill Black my fellow soldier in the basketball gyms and community, continue to march!

To my two brothers from another mother Layard Banks and Derrick Smith thanks for being with me throughout it all, matter of time!

To all my former players, soldiers, and clients thanks for allowing me to work with you. All praises to God!!

Beacon of light toward my mental health recovery shout out to Stan Tucker and Dr Bullock

INTRODUCTION

Now that American involvement in Iraq and Afghanistan is winding down, warriors are telling their stories. I'm telling my story to understand my war experiences better and to therapeutically heal my mind and soul.

My story is not about a dramatic firefight or assault mission but a personal account of a warrior citizen's deployment to Iraq as a stop-loss soldier. I share my life experiences and the impact the military had on my personal and professional life. This account is a personal reflection of my transition back into the community as a warrior citizen and as a returning citizen.

Returning from Iraq, I was disillusioned about my service, easily agitated, isolated, and frustrated. I self-medicated with alcohol, lacking appropriate coping skills. I was eventually diagnosed with post-traumatic stress disorder (PTSD) and depression.

Within a four-year period after returning to America from Iraq, I was unable to utilize past positive coping skills. My heart hardened, and my moral compass was broken. I committed bank robbery, which led to twenty-four months in federal prison.

While incarcerated, I reflected on how prior to my deployment, I was a law-abiding warrior citizen with no legal troubles. I felt the media attention of my crime created a negative image of me. However, I refused to let that mistake define my life. This motivated me to restore my life.

A significant turning point occurred during incarceration. I renewed my walk with God. I began to seriously think and write about my difficulties, which allowed me to see beyond my circumstances to my possibilities.

Throughout the book, I share thoughts and experiences about life in my community, the military, a war zone, and prison. I discuss the transition challenges I faced coming from Iraq and prison. Furthermore, I share the impact of not having adequate mental health treatment while transitioning from military service and incarceration to civilian life. This book also includes poems I wrote to express my thoughts about transitioning from Iraq and prison.

CHAPTER 1

WHAT HAPPENED?

> Either how canst thou say to thy brother, let me pull out the mote that is in thine eye, when thou thyself beholdest not the beam in your own eye? Thou hypocrite cast out first the beam out of thine own eye, and then shalt thou see clearly to pull out the mote that is in thy brother's eye.
>
> —Luke 6:42 (KJ21)

I returned to Camp Atterbury, Indiana, from Iraq in August 2006. The day was hot; however, it was nothing compared to the heat I'd left in Iraq. My mind swirled with excitement, but I was frustrated with the outprocessing experience that occurred before I could return to my home.

Camp Atterbury was also home to the Edinburgh Correctional Facility. Almost daily walking past the correctional facility, I thought how ironic. Soldiers were returning or going to war, and civilians were losing or gaining their freedom at the same time—only in America.

While outprocessing, I stood in long lines to turn in weapons and equipment. I remember feeling as if I were in a line for a roller-coaster ride, anxious to get on but once on ready for it to be over with quickly. Completing paperwork, I was just rushing to sign it, not really reading it. During debriefings, I was not listening, only daydreaming about getting back home to my family and friends.

I returned home disillusioned, feeling that my service for the country was not appreciated after watching the news and seeing how political Operation Iraqi Freedom had become with no end in sight.

Before long, my heart began to harden daily with each sunrise, causing me to turn away from God. I slowly lost focus on my life as a father, warrior citizen, social worker, coach, and mentor.

Meanwhile, during my transition home, I used bad coping skills and self-medicated with alcohol to numb my feelings. I changed from being a social, weekend drinker to secretly drinking alcohol daily. I was in denial of having an alcohol problem, believing I was functional at work and therefore, I had no problem.

After several months, family and friends noticed changes in my behavior. I became secluded, spending more time in the basement, angry all the time, cussing nonstop. I avoided going out socially. I reluctantly sought help at the vet center and the VA hospital.

Then I was diagnosed with post-traumatic stress disorder (PTSD) and depression. I participated in treatment like a swimmer diving into cold water—hesitantly. Frustrated with comments from friends and professionals to "get over it" and "move on with your life" or that "you're a social worker; you know how to get better," I stopped going to mental health treatment. I depended on my old, reliable alcohol for relief. My life slowly drifted away like a bottle in an ocean, changing me into an angry, confused, and frustrated man.

Drinking alcohol altered my mind, and I forgot about my past life accomplishments, like graduating college and becoming a warrior citizen, social worker, and mentor. I now felt alone, angry, and depressed, believing nobody understood me. In the midst of that storm, I continued to help others cope and adjust to their problems in life.

Daily, it felt as if I were boiling like an egg in hot water, unable to express myself. I began to isolate myself. I felt that my negative thoughts were eating my soul like termites slowly gnawing through wood.

Then my thoughts turned to a dark side, and I began to think of ways to get back at an uncaring world that didn't show respect for my military service. These negative thoughts turned into action, with me committing six bank robberies. The consequences of my actions led to my incarceration, only putting more wood on the fire with my frustration, depression, and anger.

Meanwhile, during incarceration, I reflected with every sunrise how I had become a person the prison industry would profit off of. I worked many years, teaching others how to avoid this hell of a modern plantation, but yet there I was. Also, I felt frustration daily with thinking how I had disgraced my family, the army, and my community by turning to crime.

A change occurred one day. While reading the Bible, I was feeling very depressed. I realized during troubling times, you have a choice how you will respond to a situation—with a spiritual mind-set or from a worldly viewpoint. Damn, my life power switch was turned on again! I had to make a choice despite my current situation in jail.

While awaiting sentencing, I continued to weigh my

options—adopting an "I don't give a damn attitude" versus focusing on God to guide and give strength toward my unseen future. I eventually renewed my faith and hoped that God would turn this bad situation into a good maturation of my life. I accepted responsibility for my actions, pleading guilty to three counts of bank robbery.

Next, God showed me grace with my federal sentencing, receiving twenty-four months. I point out my life as a warrior citizen contributed to my light sentencing. I did not have a prior criminal history, and the judge took my military and professional careers into consideration.

My sentencing gave me hope. I began believing not my power but God's power would get me through whatever occurred during my incarceration journey. Further, I had faith I could rebuild my life once released from federal prison.

While incarcerated, I planned my transition back to society, using the after-action report model I had learned in the army. Daily, I reflected on my Iraq transition home, thinking about what went well, which areas I could strengthen, and what I must eliminate to enhance success as a returning citizen.

Also, I reflected, using common sense, and realized how God was protecting me, shielding me from death and physical injuries while so many people got hurt or killed in the streets, over in Iraq, and in prison. I became grateful for being spared those things, which inspired me to do better.

Day by day, my thoughts about my life became clearer. I accepted responsibility for my negative actions. I stopped pointing fingers at others and developed the will to change, renewing my mind and heart with God through prayer, exercise, and the pursuit of knowledge. I was ready to deal with the hurt I had put on my family by preparing to do better coping with my anger.

In addition, a new life seed was planted in me during my incarceration, the Alcoholics Anonymous (AA) Twelve-Step program, which I learned to use as a new coping tool. However, I still didn't believe I was an alcoholic at that time. Alcohol clouded my vision with the desire to drink, and I felt social drinking would be okay once I was released from prison.

Reality hit me near the end of my federal incarceration. I was looking at more legal issues with pending Maryland state charges and a divorce once released from federal custody. These situations had me nervous. It felt like I was walking on a tightrope high in the sky. My feelings of anger and frustration returned. I was feeling like a person who file their taxes on time expecting money back but still owe the government. The difference was this time, I trusted God to guide me through these situations.

After my release from federal prison, within four months, I was found not guilty by trial on Maryland state charges. In eight months, I reached a divorce agreement. Whew, finally taking a deep breath, sitting alone, I thought, *I can now begin to rebuild my life.*

During the transition from prison to supervised release, I began to execute again like a warrior citizen. I sincerely participated in PTSD treatment at the VA hospital and vet center. I took my life experiences seriously and applied the new awareness and coping skills to my life daily.

After several months working small jobs and my mental health improving, I applied to jobs matching my skill set of counseling.

I eventually regained a professional job working with the homeless population two years after my release from prison. Also, I remarried three years after release from prison to a wonderful, caring woman. I began to feel loved again, and my self-esteem returned. I really felt productive again and ready for my new life journey.

Two years into my marriage, I was feeling optimistic about my life direction; however, I relaxed about attending PTSD groups and began drinking alcohol again regularly. I was like the Bible verse in Proverbs 26:11 (KJ21), "As a dog returnth to his vomit, so a fool returneth to his folly."

The difference with this relapse though was I maintained good communication with my wife, and I sincerely expressed myself with my vet center social worker. Both of them normalized my feelings but encouraged me to re-address my coping skills for handling stress and take my mental health issues more seriously. I returned to participating in regular treatment again, hoping to steady my lifeboat in this rough sea of life.

This time in treatment, I learned how my PTSD symptoms impacted me and my work performance and how my reaction to stress caused me more life problems. For example, work stress and being unable to complete work assignments in a timely manner caused me to be depressed. Also, being unable to concentrate and having difficulty sitting through meetings caused me to become frustrated and easily agitated by my inability to function normally like I did before my Iraq deployment.

I fought daily like a boxing sparring partner not to crash emotionally. Also, I struggled with holding off my negative thoughts again. I reluctantly acknowledged I needed to readdress my mental health full-time to maintain a productive life.

Meanwhile, with a new commitment to living a productive life, I realized I had to make changes. I resigned from my homeless program job with my wife's support and understanding.

Further, my vet center social worker and I thought that a

less demanding, less stressful work situation, one in which I was not helping others through their problems but addressing mine, would help improve my mental health.

My vet center social worker explained it to me in a military manner. The example was how a soldier would react to a gas or nerve agent. First, the soldier would put on his or her gas mask and administer the atropine injection first before helping others. For the first time, I realized the need for self-help in order to be available physically, mentally, and emotionally to help others.

While making these life changes, I explored working different jobs, such as food delivery and ride sharing to supplement my disability pay. It was less stressful for me—no paperwork, just focusing on safety and driving to my destination. Plus, I had the option to work my own hours.

"Matter of time" moment—I felt this work option reduced stress, enhancing my mental health, and therefore changed my work career.

Another "matter of time" moment occurred five days after I resigned from my homeless program job. One night out drinking heavily again, I literally crashed. My excuse to drink was to cope with a close friend's death.

During this drunken relapse, I had an automobile accident because of road rage. I had a flashback of my Iraq convoy experiences triggered by being boxed in by traffic.

The accident situation occurred while I was driving on a one-way street. I became angry at a car ahead of me for not driving through the intersection before the light turned red.

When the light changed green, I sped around the car in front of me. While I was driving up a one-way street with cars parked on both sides of the street, a car ahead pulled out of a parking space, blocking my path. In my drunken rage, I believed I was being trapped. My Iraq convoy training instincts kicked in, and I rammed the car pulling out of the parking spot ahead out of my way. I continued up the street while the other car was still following me. I then turned and drove through an alley, trying to lose the car behind me. While turning out of the alley onto another one-way street, I crashed into a parked car and a motorcycle, and my car came to a stop.

After police came to the crash scene, I heard nobody was hurt. Neither was I. I immediately thanked God. I also thanked God for car insurance, so whatever damage I'd done, it could be fixed. However, I totaled my vehicle and was charged with DUI.

In reflection, this was my third DUI. The two previous DUI arrests occurred while I was on military duty—one in the eighties, the other in the nineties. I was embarrassed, depressed, frustrated, and disappointed with my actions again. It opened my eyes that I was an alcoholic! My life was unmanageable. At the police station, I remembered the twelve-step seed planted while I was in prison.

The next day, I decided to seek treatment in the substance and alcohol abuse program at the VA hospital. I thought, *Stop faking. Be straight up. Handle your business, soldier, so you can continue to march.*

Finally, I entered and completed the outpatient and aftercare program at the VA hospital. Now, daily, I strive to take it one day at a time, maintaining my sobriety and continuing regular PTSD treatment. Now I'm marching one day at a time.

CHAPTER 2

THE BEGINNING

My life story begins in Washington, DC, where I was born at Freeman's Hospital. I grew up in northwest DC, "uptown." My early childhood memories are filled with being proud of my neighborhood, excited about life, and full of adventure.

I am the only child. My father was a US Marine veteran who worked numerous jobs, including as a security guard at Walter Reed Army Hospital and as a plasterer by trade, as well as odd jobs. He taught plastering and drywall at Lorton Prison for DC offenders. My mother was a registered nurse at Saint Elizabeth's Mental Health Hospital. Both of my parents instilled in me the desire to "make it" by education and the belief that I was special.

I remember my father working two jobs throughout my childhood, always encouraging me to pursue an education and participate in sports. My mother expected nothing but the best from me and for me to be a leader and a good man in my community. From an early age, I strived to make them proud of me.

I had two remarkable grandmothers, my paternal grandmother, Mama Mac, and my maternal grandmother, Granny. Mama Mac lived in Atlanta, Georgia, and Granny lived in Indianapolis, Indiana. Both were very spiritual women and had great influence on my spiritual life.

I visited Granny on holidays and summers for a few days, but she visited DC often, staying for a month at a time during my childhood. Granny was calm and soft-spoken and could cook some good fried chicken! Also, she always encouraged me to be respectful to all adults and said that I could achieve anything if I put my mind to it.

I visited Mama Mac every summer from age nine to thirteen. She spoiled me and boosted my self-esteem, always telling me I was smart and how proud she was of me. Even if I did wrong, she would always make it seem all right by saying, "Learn from your mistakes." Reflecting back, I can see I was blessed with a loving family full of encouragement.

Now don't get it twisted; my family had issues and wasn't perfect, but I had a solid, hardworking family who mirrored the success opportunities of black people during the 1960s and '70s.

My home was in the heart of "uptown," northwest DC. I lived one block off Georgia Avenue near Howard University and three blocks from Fourteenth Street.

Growing up, I saw college students, hardworking adults in the legal field, number runners, drug dealers and users, boosters, pimps, bank robbers, and prostitutes all during the exciting, turbulent time of the late 1960s and the '70s with civil rights, black nationalism, and the Vietnam war era in full blast.

My view of black people was that we were a strong, smart people determined to overcome slavery and discrimination since being brought over from Africa to America. James Brown captured the feeling with his song, "Say It Loud—I'm Black and Proud."

Growing up in DC, "Chocolate City," my worldview wasn't how it really was in the world. I thought blacks were the majority and whites the minority, the DC view. However, in reality, it was a white majority and black minority national view. Some cities and states didn't have high government or professional people of color in power yet.

One person who shaped this DC view and impacted my life was Mayor Marion Barry. His summer youth job program provided my first work experience, and he was responsible for providing many services to the people in my community.

Later on, Mayor Barry faced life challenges and revived his personal and political life. Further, he showed how to rebuild your life as a returning citizen. This inspired me when I became a returning citizen. RIP Mayor Barry!

In my neighborhood, all of the children on the block grew up like family. We went in and out of each other's homes, eating each other's food. We had cookouts and parties to which all on the block were welcome. Even though I was the only child, it was like I grew up with all these brothers and sisters.

Also, the adult men and women on my block went to work daily, providing for their families. They always encouraged all of the youths on the block to make something good out of our lives.

There were many events, situations, and life teachings that shaped my development; however, I view my sports participation as the main catalyst in shaping me. I played football, basketball, and baseball at my neighborhood recreation center, Raymond Playground, and with the Police Boys and Girls Club Numbers 10 and 6. Also, I played high school football and ran track. I briefly ran track in college too.

Before long, participation in sports was the foundation of my mental and physical toughness. I learned how to deal with success and failure through sports. In hindsight, sports prepared me for my life journey.

I feel sports shaped and channeled my aggression into socially accepted actions. For instance, in football, if you make a good hard hit, people clap for you. Now, make a hard hit to somebody walking down the street and you get arrested or hurt. Further, I learned how to read as a youth by reading the sports page daily because of my interest in sports.

Also, I gained self-esteem and peer acceptance through sports participation in neighborhood games and leagues around the city. The love of sports has always been my grounding point and source of self-esteem and accomplishment.

Next, I learned about street life, from observing the older neighborhood guys, whom my peers and I tried to emulate. However, the older guys always stressed the importance of getting an education too. They encouraged and supported my participation in sports and then later attending and completing college. The old saying "Do as I say, not what I do" occurred often in my life.

I was exposed to urban drama (drug overdoses, murder) in my neighborhood and saw peers locked up for stealing and hustling drugs. In hindsight, this was my first experience with PTSD without knowing it at the time.

At this point, I've chosen not to go any further in depth about life in my hood. I believe the negative actions and consequences of brothers and sisters are due to the slave mentality, which the American system created to keep us misled.

Further, alcohol, drugs, and miseducation cause some not to conduct their lives in a positive, law-abiding manner. Therefore, I'm not going to dramatize misery or glamorize that part of my life experiences. Let's continue to march on with this story.

CHAPTER 3

MEANING OF MATTER OF TIME

Reflecting back on my life experiences, I see that alcohol and drug usage were normal activities in my community, at college, and in the military. I had to learn by trial and error the benefits and consequences of usage.

There was one partying session that affected my life course. It was in 1984, when I was given the nickname of "Matter of Time," while watching one of NFL's hottest rivalry games, the Washington Redskins versus the Dallas Cowboys, with friends. Now, this game is big in DC. People held game parties and planned family gatherings around this game.

I remember some of my friends watching the game. We were in our early twenties doing what young men our age did—talking trash, eating food, and drinking beer. During the game, Redskins and Cowboys fans were going back and forth verbally, play by play, arguing who was going to win. We were cheering like we were live at the stadium.

The Redskins were losing in the second and third quarter, and I kept saying, "It's a matter of time before the Redskins come back and win." In the fourth quarter, the Redskins were still losing, but I kept saying, "Matter of time."

One guy kept saying, "Matter of time, huh? Skins getting whupped."

The game ended, and the Redskins lost, but we continued enjoying the rest of the night.

The next day, I saw my friends, and the Cowboys fans were laughing at me about the game. One friend walked up and said, "Wassup, Matter of Time?" From that day on, some people in the hood just started calling me "Matter of Time."

Before long, the self-fulfilling prophecy occurred with me being called "Matter of Time"—but in a negative manner.

My attitude and behavior, especially while under the influence of alcohol and drugs, were outrageous. I began to act out in the community, at clubs and go-go's, and at house parties. I would attempt to eat all the food and drink as much alcohol, especially beer, as I could at parties. That led to people saying, "Here come shorty, Matter of Time." It was funny to me at first, until I realized how out of control I was.

A turning point occurred one night. I lunched out, drinking beer and smoking PCP, "love boat." I remember being in an apartment building with everybody when an altercation happened. I tried to break it up, and then I just ran off down the street.

That next morning, I remember waking up lying in a yard not remembering anything. I thought, *Damn! My first blackout.* After returning home, sleeping, and showering up. I found out from a friend that I had tried to stop an argument and began yelling, "Nobody don't understand." Then I just took off running. He said everybody was laughing, saying, "Look at Matter of Time."

Next, I remember feeling like a person performing in a play having stage fright and forgetting my lines—embarrassed. I thought about my life direction. At the time, I was attending

Howard University, in the army reserve, and a father of two. I felt this was not my purpose in life, getting high, drunk, and being irresponsible, acting like a fool in the community.

That day, I then committed myself to limiting my drug and alcohol usage. I could be a functional user, like many in society—or so I thought. My goal was not to hinder my progress in college, work, and military duty.

Another driving force to change was that I viewed fatherhood as very important. I remember how my father encouraged me, stressing that spending time with, teaching, and guiding my children were as important as providing financially for them. I decided to be a responsible father to my children, being actively involved in their life development. Further, I realized my actions didn't just impact me but them too, so I changed.

My journey after this "matter of time" moment during the next four years continued with a can-do army attitude I learned being a warrior citizen. I continued college as a responsible man working a full-time job.

A couple of years later, I finally graduated from Howard University in 1985 with a BSW and in 1988 with an MSW. Reaching these milestones, I believed a higher power helped me to navigate the DC streets, college, work, and fatherhood all while being a warrior citizen in the army reserve.

I remember feeling proud of my accomplishment and excited about starting my career as a social worker. I believed that my success happened in a "matter of time," by God's grace and mercy.

Next, in my professional, community, and coaching efforts, I named programs and youth basketball teams I led "Matter of Time" to honor how God blessed me despite my youthful mistakes.

I believe life takes us all through different phases, seasons, and trials that we all will encounter in a "matter of time." Now the completion of this book adds another season to the "matter of time" regarding my life.

Matter of Time Poem

Matter of time ain't no rhyme; it's about your mind. How you learn and grow, God already knows. In a matter of time, you will develop that mind.

See that's what I do; I conspire to inspire my people to go higher. I'm deacon of the ghetto from DC streets, old school go-go beat; don't be afraid of the drum; come get this knowledge, son!

What's up in the hood, it's not all good. People fuss, fight and kill, smoke crack, weed, drink liquor, wine, and gamble all the time. Youngins playing sports, running and gunning, but who is developing their mind. Yeah that's right, matter of time!

If you use your time and expand your mind, one will truly find God's treasure inside. Don't be afraid to try, and don't let failures tell you to stop. Keep pushing to learn. Never stop yearning for that burning desire to reach higher! See how matter of time inspires. At the end of the day, ask yourself did you compete, work to be the best, apply positive use of your ability. Whatever the answer, hopefully you live another day to try it again. Matter of time encourages you to be God's friend.

Don't forget it's a time to live, a time to eat, a time to love; now it's a matter of time to stay focused! To improve your mind so you won't be left behind!

—CTF Jail, 2010

CHAPTER 4

MILITARY

The military gave me exposure to different races. It taught me discipline and confidence to perform any task and gave me leadership opportunities.

My first opinion of the military was from my father, who was a Montford Point Marine. The Montford Point Marines were an all-black World War II unit. He instilled in me the importance of being neat, well groomed, and independent. I learned to wash and iron my clothes and cook and developed a strong work ethic.

I remember asking my father how he got that work ethic. He credited his daily work ethic and toughness to the Marine Corps and growing up poor. Observing my father shaped the first image of the military for me.

My first contact with the military was during the 1968 riots when Martin Luther King Jr. was murdered. I remembered walking to school seeing soldiers in green uniforms, which I liked, on the corner with M-16s. I remember seeing the older neighborhood youngsters throwing rocks and calling them names, "da pigs," to see if they would leave the corner and chase them. To my surprise, the soldiers remained disciplined and stayed on the corner. At a young age, that impressed me.

When I became older, I realized that was discipline being displayed before me.

Also, I watched men from my community returning home from Vietnam during the 1970s, being misunderstood and turning to drugs and crime. However, many others returned and became productive, working government jobs or as metro bus drivers and so on too.

In reflection, I can see that the Vietnam vets in my community were strong men who could overcome racism to work jobs and raise their families despite their faults. I grew up believing these soldiers were overcomers in life because of their military training. It gave me hope that I could achieve anything I put my mind to too.

Finally, I accepted the challenge to enlist in the army as a teenage father during the early 1980s while in college. My thought was it meant a steady income, benefits, and career options versus being a hustler and selling drugs, which could lead to incarceration or death. For me, the military made more sense.

Many years later, after my deployment from Iraq, I would experience the pain and difficulty with re-adjusting to the community and my family as a war veteran. The Vietnam veterans' transition was done without the services that are offered and available now. I salute those soldiers for persevering despite those obstacles. *Continue to march.*

CHAPTER 5

YOU'RE IN THE ARMY NOW

In 1980, I was a student at Virginia State University living on campus, deciding my daily options, whether to go to class or hang out. Often, I did a combination of both, hanging out with my DC friends, drinking, partying, and jamming with Trouble Funk, EU, and Rare Essence go-go bands' cassette tapes; going to class and parties; and playing sports.

While attending Virginia State for two years, I learned how to become a better student and gave serious thought to my life choices. I remember feeling blessed being in college and not in DC with the lure of street life and hustling. Also, I didn't have to deal with the daily violence and destruction it brought in my community back in DC.

My sophomore year, I was a father of one with another child due in April. I was wondering how I would support and care for two children at nineteen going on twenty years old. Where would I work to provide for them? Could I finish college? Should I quit school and hustle or sell drugs?

One morning, I decided I would join the army, thinking of my father's military career and the neighborhood military veterans who were able to provide for and guide their families.

Meanwhile, I called my paternal grandmother, Mama Mac,

telling her first of my plans of joining the army. I remember Mama Mac praying with me over the phone, advising me to be a good, responsible father and continue to pursue my education. Whatever decision I made, she would be behind me. Her support meant a lot to me. I visited an army recruiter with the plan to go into the active army. I didn't tell anyone else of my thoughts of joining the military for a couple of weeks. Now the tough part was telling my parents about my decision to join the military.

Both of my parents were surprised about me wanting to stop attending college and join the military. They respected my decision but insisted I complete college too. However, I remember my father being upset with me for joining the army instead of the marines. He called the army "Boy Scouts."

A matter of time moment—I was inducted into the army in Richmond, Virginia however, the day before signing up, I reluctantly called my father. Our conversation made me realize my options better. I could continue my education by joining the army reserve, return home, and then transfer to attend college, either Howard University or the University of the District of Columbia (UDC) College, and be involved with my children instead of enlisting in active duty. Further, my father explained, it would be better being in DC, managing my relationships with them instead of doing it far away at a military base away from family.

I thought about that during the night before my induction into the army, and I changed my decision of going active duty, instead joining the army reserve. On reflection, I can see I was blessed with wise counsel by my father.

The next day, my recruiter was upset with having to change my paperwork to split option training for basic and advanced individual (AIT) training. Typewriter days!

After I was sworn into the army on March 19,1982, in Richmond, Virginia. I was assigned to the 310th TAACOM Ft. Belvoir Reserve unit. I was scheduled for basic training on June 4, 1982, and AIT in June 1983 during my college summer break. I was in the army reserve—a real life changer for me.

CHAPTER 6

LEARNING IN BASIC

I went to basic training at Ft. Knox, Kentucky, in June 1982, getting down to the song "Early in the Morning" by the Gap Band. Once at basic training, the song took on new meaning with waking up at 3:30 a.m.

My drill sergeant, a Vietnam veteran, was a tough instructor who instilled teamwork and knowing task, condition, and standard. Also, he stressed properly executing all soldier tasks. Further, he always wore starched uniforms with his boots shined so well you could see yourself.

I remember one example of how Drill Sergeant taught our platoon teamwork. Every squad had an area to clean in barracks. He would discipline the whole platoon if barracks was not cleaned to his standard, never singling out one squad that was not performing to standard. Further, if he noticed a particular soldier doing all the work, like buffing the floor, he provided remedial training. We all did push-ups, with him saying, "Everybody has to be able to perform all tasks to standard."

Also, Drill Sergeant would say, "We are only as strong as our weakest link." Therefore, everybody would be strong. Then came the command, "Front lean and rest position, move!" Plus, he encouraged us to assist one another in any weak areas and not to point fingers at each other. Then we all did push-ups again!

Before long, I remember the platoon jelling and assisting each other with shining boots, drill, and ceremonies and encouraging soldiers who were in worse physical shape to work out in the barracks.

I learned a life lesson in basic training from Drill Sergeant about being able to work with all races. Growing up in DC, "Chocolate City," I was around more blacks than any other race. In the military, I was living and working with people of all races who grew up in different parts of the country.

One incident that shaped me for life was I entered the army as a private first class (PFC) because of my college credits. Drill Sergeant didn't let me put my rank on because he said I hadn't earned it with not completing basic training yet.

However, I got paid as a PFC, so I didn't care, but I became upset with not being put in a leadership position. I felt the reason was that I was black. All squad leaders were white soldiers. I was on my Black Panther, black power shit, feeling it was racist but not speaking on it. I quickly became motivated and determined to do well but was ashamed with not speaking out about this perceived slight.

Another situation in basic that shaped me was being bunked in a four-man room not in the open bay. I was the only black person in the room. This arrangement was a cultural shock for us all and was orchestrated by Drill Sergeant. We were all from different areas of the country—South Dakota, Iowa, Kentucky, and me from DC. There was tension in the room the first few days, mainly coming from me not talking to any of them unless I had to.

About two weeks in, I became upset with the South Dakota

soldier because he seemed to stare at me. One night, I asked him, "What are you staring at?"

He replied, "I never saw a black man in person before basic training."

I jumped up and told him, "If you keep staring, you will see a black man kick your ass."

My bunk mate from Kentucky came between us. We were all pushing, yelling, and cussing. Drill Sergeant came into the room and instructed me to go to his office, which I did, furious.

In the office, Drill Sergeant told me I thought I was bad since I was from DC. He said if I wanted to fight someone, I could fight him. I stood there frozen, not knowing what to do. Then Drill Sergeant told me everybody was green and the US Army patch stood for "US" in these damn uniforms; therefore, we worked together! Then he told me I was selfish, but I had the potential to be a good soldier once I learned selfless service. Drill Sergeant walked me back into the four-man room saying, "Any more problems you're all going home after I kick your ass." Needless to say, we all went to sleep.

The next morning, to my surprise, in formation, Drill Sergeant made me squad leader. I was shocked. The responsibility of being squad leader changed me. I began developing better working relationships with all races throughout basic training. I learned how to work with others, being a leader and a well-rounded soldier.

After graduation, Drill Sergeant told me I would be a good soldier and he was expecting greatness in my life. "Drive on." I felt so proud! I often reflect on my basic training experiences as a building block to becoming a good soldier, social worker, coach, and mentor.

Throughout my military career, I enjoyed traveling and meeting different people of all races.

I credit basic training with giving me more confidence to finish college and work a full-time job as a young father.

Another major military accomplishment besides basic training was graduating from drill sergeant school in 1990. I served nine years as an army reserve drill sergeant, which paralleled with my professional social work and coaching success.

My army career lasted twenty-four years. I served as an infantry soldier, supply soldier, drill sergeant, classroom instructor, basic noncommissioned officer (BNOC), advanced noncommissioned officer (ANOC), and small group instructor.

Finally, I remember during my deployment to Iraq in 2005–06, I appreciated my basic training drill sergeant for preparing me to be a leader in a war environment as a *green US Army soldier*!

CHAPTER 7

AMERICAN DREAM?

I believed the "American dream" was rising from DC city life and living in a four-bedroom, two-car garage home and having a family who loved me, life happily ever after, a storybook ending.

Further, I felt despite our country's flaws, people around the world wanted to come to the United States to live and raise their families. Our country gives an opportunity to inspire and achieve your dreams (business, jobs, home). Our infrastructure (electricity, water, roads, and so on) is the best worldwide. Plus, we have a democratic government, which although flawed, gives people the opportunity to vote for our leaders that other countries aspire to obtain.

I felt living in the United States, being a college graduate and an army reserve soldier, and working a government job, my life was productive. I had an optimistic worldview and expected continued life growth.

My "American dream" changed when I went to Iraq (Operation Iraqi Freedom 2005–06) at forty-two years old, a grown-ass man, and that is when my nightmare began.

I saw how civilians and soldiers are used as pawns to

achieve the interest of a select few with the vision of protecting our country from terrorist attacks.

Further, I observed how a country can influence another country with their views and governmental style, train them, and provide weapons with the intent to assist but really only to expand their interest in a foreign region.

Now, don't get it twisted; some good does come out of it for a select few in those countries. Some people are assisted to obtain positions of power, but ultimately, greed and power cause corruption while services, goods, and jobs are not distributed to the mass of their population.

Meanwhile, over in Iraq, seeing the world game being played, I was paying attention. However, this raw exposure of information impacted me in an unhealthy manner. I became angry because my efforts in Iraq seemed not to make a difference in terms of positive change. The conflict continued with IEDs, suicide bombings, and sectarian fighting.

Also, my duty stations experienced the constant threat of danger with mortar rounds. The Iraqis I worked with and trained wanted us to leave their country. For instance, I remember an Iraqi contractor saying, "You US got Saddam out; now we can govern ourselves." That conversation made a lasting impression on me regarding our purpose with being over in Iraq.

I returned to the United States disillusioned about my service making a better Iraq. There was no decrease in violence in Iraq, and their government was rife with corruption. Before long, I was having nightmares from war-zone experiences—mortar rounds, the threat of being shot at, and IED attacks while on convoy.

My early dreams consisted of things I observed—American

and Iraqi soldiers and civilians losing their lives, body parts, and minds.

Further, I was frustrated in Iraq and back in the United States with operating and abiding by the rules of engagement while the enemy (terrorists) were not operating under any rules, attacking whenever they could. This only caused me anger. These experiences especially had me agitated anytime US troops were assaulted, attacked, or blown up by IEDs. I often wondered why we didn't just get at them and punish whomever and wherever.

When I returned home, the perception of my view of conditions in my community changed. I viewed murders, joblessness, and lack of resources affecting my community differently. I started to notice only a select few benefiting, just like in Iraq. I began thinking, *How did my family and country benefit with me over in Iraq?* These thoughts swirled in my head constantly!

I remember thinking about how certain businesses and people of power profited from war's misery and death and further, how people, through government contracts, profited and how some just straight up took from people in a weaker condition.

Also, my view of the community changed too, seeing how people of color were being systematically moved out of urban city areas (gentrification), the continued violence against each other in the community (battlefield conditions), and confusion with how to educate our youth (charter versus public schools). I struggled with how I fit into my community and family again after my Iraq experiences.

While over in Iraq, I envisioned a movie script ending, returning a hero and being respected in the community. Instead, the opposite occurred. My high school basketball coaching job was not available for the next season. They made the decision to give the job back to staff in the school building while I was in Iraq. I was thinking, *Damn, you're fired! There was no indication of change before I deployed; now a coaching change was made?* I concluded my being over in Iraq for a year was the reason; therefore, I felt I was being penalized for my service to the country.

Another situation that impacted me negatively was the difficulty I faced renewing my social work license. My license had expired while I was deployed in Iraq. I felt the board should renew my license and waive continuing education classes. I thought that I should be allowed to start anew as a social worker with two years to complete continuing education classes since I was deployed to Iraq. However, I was required to complete continuing education classes within a year for license renewal.

In hindsight, I can see that at this time, my thoughts about complying with the standards were not rational. I thought my license should have been renewed, waiving continuing education. I seethed with anger and reluctantly completed the requirements. I felt that this was my punishment for being deployed to Iraq.

Finally, I developed a "Why me?" attitude. I seemed trapped in this nightmare as a middle-aged man with a family, professionally employed and, I thought, respected in my community. However, I felt God had forsaken me. Plus, nobody understood or cared about my sacrifice being a warrior citizen.

I began to have a different concept of the "American dream." I felt it was vanity, the futile emptiness of trying to be happy apart from God, like Solomon in the Bible book of Ecclesiastes. I was in my "matter of time" despair mode.

My nightmare continued for four years. I felt disconnected from God. I acted on my bad thoughts, which led me to be incarcerated. Finally, I woke up! Reality hit. I became a black man facing what I had worked all my life and encouraged others to avoid, incarceration. *Damn*!

DC Invisible Man Poem

City changing, I'm trying to maintain, nothing looking the same, trying not to go insane I walk the street receptive to greet but people look straight through me like, don't have time to meet "wow." Should I care?

Still I push! I walk with a stare, feeling like stranger beware. Then I think how it used to be all black, but had to beware of an attack, black on black crime. Despite it all I felt safe in my hood. Love was around, black power, do for self, one love but now it seems gone.

Gentrification is what's happening in the nation. Don't have to look far; it's on my block! Push out the poor, trick the sick, sell their house for the cash, got damn 10% creating a monopoly. They price you out, and they don't hear your shouts! In the '60s–'70s, they moved out. Now they push us out or we sell, then can't get back, what the hell?

My people don't have nothing only bluffing can't stand together especially during bad weather. Turn against one another, what's going on my sisters and brothers? It's been done since we were brought here from Africa as slaves, divide and conquer, got damn Willie Lynch still getting paid!

Let's get to the point; as a vet, people say thanks for your service and we appreciate you, then show you different, family luv u but don't understand, just know they still luv u man. VA services slow then they say, you know how it goes hurry up wait. It's the same with claims. Try not to go insane, medication given like candy on Halloween, PTSD treatment cool but sometimes feel like a fool, you lose your cool, taught methods to cope. Soldier, don't give up hope!

Jesse Jackson used to say, "I am somebody." Does anybody see me? Why won't they reinstate my claim? Is it complicated to request, reinstate benefits and review for increase? Good grief!

I waited a year for it all to be done. It made me crazier, son. I moved on with my life focus not to lose sight. Don't put trust in man. Have faith in God while he unveil his plan. I learned to trust God! But trust me, at times, it's hard but God always works it out.

Take my advice; read Proverbs and Psalms. It will help you keep on keeping on! Then you might see how God will direct your life. Sit back, relax, drink a Sprite. Be ready for another day after night, sure you right!

—August 2013 supervised release

CHAPTER 8

STOP-LOSS DEPLOYMENT

In January 2005, the Eightieth Division had a drill weekend duty where all attached battalions met at headquarters in Richmond, Virginia. I sensed, like most soldiers in the unit, that the division would be mobilized to go to Iraq. Well, sure enough, that is what happened. Attention to orders; the Eightieth Division will be mobilized to go to Operation Iraqi Freedom.

Now with twenty-three years in the army reserve coming to an end, I thought, *Now this*. It was ironic. I was due to retire in November 2005. My service continued for another year as a stop-loss soldier.

Personally, the timing was not good for me. All four of my children were at a critical stage of development, and my parents were both in their eighties and their health and levels of functioning were declining, which had me concerned about their care.

Professionally, all was going well. I was a school social worker, led a male mentoring program and a high school basketball coach. I had been planting positive seeds in the community for the past ten years and was feeling proud of my accomplishments. I felt only greater things would happen, but I had an interruption with this deployment.

I remember reflectively thinking I'd joined the army voluntarily in 1982, knowing this possibility existed with defending my country. I thought about how after receiving training and money for many years, I had to go fulfill my obligation and earn that pay.

Being a stop-loss soldier impacted me mentally and emotionally. I questioned my loyalty to the country. How would this deployment help me and my family? I was due to retire yet was not allowed. However, army ethics instilled throughout the years overrode my concerns. I reluctantly refocused on fulfilling my commitment to the best of my ability.

I told my family of my upcoming deployment. Then I noticed the apprehension from my family members about me going to Iraq. Over the next few months, my family and I monitored the news of Iraq more closely with what was going on "over there."

Then a matter of time moment occurred. My orders changed with my unit tasked to operate an accelerated drill sergeant academy from April to June for Eightieth Division soldiers. I received orders assigning me to this mission; therefore, I wasn't going to Iraq!

I remember thinking, *This is how a person feels being diagnosed with cancer but then being told the tumor is benign not malignant—overjoyed*. Whew! After taking a deep breath, I was ready for active duty in country.

However, I would still be on military leave from my job while on active duty at the drill sergeant academy, stationed at Ft. A. P. Hill, Virginia. I was still close to home and able to visit family when off duty or on weekends.

Also, I was still able to monitor my basketball team's

off-season workouts with my coaches, and I could still observe some summer league games too. I felt blessed that I was able to continue my life personally and professionally. Strangely, my thoughts became conflicted about not going to Iraq. I wanted to go with my Eightieth Division soldiers to Iraq.

CHAPTER 9

REPORTING TO FORT A. P. HILL

When I reported to A. P. Hill, I soon realized that my duty assignment would be an issue. I had been in my new unit for four months, training to be an instructor at the drill sergeant academy. I had to complete a certification training requirement; however, the class was discontinued. At the time of deployment, I had only completed three months out of a twelve-month course. Because of being mobilized for this mission, I wouldn't be able to complete the course.

My concern was what my duty assignment would be. I was thinking, *You have been a drill sergeant longer than most instructors in your unit but are not certified to instruct at drill sergeant academy, so now what will your duty position be?*

Next, I remember command reviewing my 201 personnel file record, and they saw I had a supply MOS (military occupational specialty) 76Y. I was assigned to the supply room; however, I would be consulted when needed by other instructors with any issues that might occur during training. I was thinking, *Yeah right, not holding my breath for that.*

I was skeptical about the supply assignment, because I hadn't worked in that capacity in fifteen years, and I wanted to be an instructor to better utilize my skill set. Then I thought,

I'm not going to Iraq. I'm still close to my family, and upon completion of academy graduation, I will return home to my family and coach my team.

Then I felt God was working things out for me. Like Proverbs 3:7 (KJ21) says, "Trust in the Lord and lean not upon your understanding." Later on, my faith would be tested with this scripture, little did I know.

During the mission, everything was going well. The supply sergeant and I worked well together, and it was less stressful than being an instructor. I monitored my family and basketball team with daily phone calls and visits back to DC when off.

I even conducted a one-day basketball clinic, and I was scheduled to work a basketball summer camp session. Also, I was going to work at a university basketball summer camp once I completed my training mission too. I was excited about the basketball opportunities and being recognized as an up-and-coming coach in the DC area.

At this time, I believed I would retire from the army in November, continue my employment in the school system as a special education social worker, coach basketball, and continue guiding my family at home where I belonged.

Then a matter of time moment started brewing during the last two weeks of training. There were rumors that more soldiers from the Eightieth Division would be deployed to Iraq because of some problems with soldiers completing training and health concerns.

The rumor at A. P. Hill was that some of us would be mobilized after graduation. I became nervous and conflicted, wondering if I would be selected, but I wanted to go too. I was thinking, *Why do you want to go to Iraq?* These feelings bothered me, not knowing the reason, so one day, I went to command, asking if I was going to be deployed. I was told the drill sergeant academy mission to which I was assigned would continue and was still essential to Eightieth Division's overall mission of providing training to the region.

I remember stressing that I needed to know because of my basketball commitments at camps and, most important, to prepare my family and myself for going to Iraq. Command stated at that time that I was not going to Iraq.

On June 5, 2005, the drill sergeant academy graduation was held. I returned home excited about being with my family and looking forward to working basketball camps and coaching my team during the summer.

I wasn't home four hours when, while at a restaurant, my twin daughter called me and said, "Your command called and asked for you to call immediately." I wondered why they had called me. I was around command all morning and during graduation.

Finally, I reluctantly returned the call, and I was told, "You are deployed to Iraq. Orders are being mailed, and you need to report to Camp Atterbury, Indiana, for training in two weeks."

I was shocked and angry at the short time of preparing my family mentally and emotionally and notifying my job before report date.

I expressed my concern and was given an additional week to finalize my personal, professional, and business situations before reporting to Camp Atterbury. Things were moving fast. There was anxiety with family, friends, and myself regarding the upcoming tour of duty in Iraq.

That night, I remember thinking about that Bible verse again: "Trust in the Lord, lean not your own understanding" (Proverbs 3:7 KJ21). Now, I thought, *You are going have to walk it like you talk it.*

CHAPTER 10

CAMP ATTERBURY

I said my goodbyes to family and friends, and I flew out of Baltimore Washington International Airport on July 5, 2005. While walking through the airport, I became focused on learning the new skills I needed to survive in Iraq.

Once at the gate, while waiting to board the airplane, my mind began to race with the unknown that awaited me over there. Then I saw my battle buddy Sergeant Bemore, who was in my ANOC and BNOC instructor unit the past five years. We greeted each other, and he started laughing. He said, "Your ass going to Iraq, soldier." Sergeant Bemore was home for Fourth of July pass and now on his way back to Camp Atterbury too.

During the flight, Sergeant Bemore told me what to expect at Camp Atterbury, and he told me who else was up there. All my anxiety left while I was talking with Sergeant Bemore.

Once at Camp Atterbury, after getting assigned to F company and receiving equipment and weapons—a nine millimeter and M-4 rifle—I realized this shit was real. I got settled and began training. The only adjustment I had to make was getting used to wearing my body armor (battle rattle) especially while firing my M-4 and nine-millimeter. I quickly made the adjustment, qualifying with firing weapons and completing all training requirements.

Bemore and I normally met up after training to chill and process the day of training. Bemore knew what his Iraq assignment was going to be, convoy team, while I wasn't given an assignment yet, which only made me more upset with command.

In reflection, my issue was I was being encouraged to put in a promotion packet for E-8 after a week at Camp Atterbury, and I refused. My thinking was I was in stop-loss status, and I wanted to retire once the tour was completed; therefore, I wanted no obligation to remain in the army reserve, possibly for another year after deployment.

Another issue complicating my duty assignment was my experience as a drill sergeant and classroom instructor and my infantry MOS. Further, it seemed my education level—a master's degree and being a social worker—was making it a difficult decision where to place me during this deployment.

Eventually, command told me, "You will be placed into an E-8 position, so you might as well put in the promotion packet to get paid more and retire with a higher pay grade." I still maintained my position of not submitting the promotion packet then and throughout my tour, so I could retire when I returned from Iraq.

In hindsight, this is when I perceived my issues began with command making my deployment difficult and political.

Word got out that deployment to Iraq would begin in August, and I was on the first lift (1b) to Kuwait for additional training in country. My man Bemore was shipping out on first lift (1a).

Before arriving in Iraq, we went to Kuwait for additional training and acclimation to the weather. The training was held for a minimum of one week. Now my duty assignment was given to me. I was placed in a supply MOS position. They told me my leadership skills were needed as a first sergeant at a base in Al Kasik, Iraq. I had not actively worked in supply since 1989, even though I was just in a supply job recently at drill sergeant academy for six weeks. I remember thinking, *Just drive on. Get this deployment over, and return home to your family.*

CHAPTER 11

KUWAIT

Once in Kuwait, walking off the plane, the first thing I noticed was the heat. It felt like a hair dryer blowing constantly on you, but the crazy thing was it was one in the morning. I was thinking, *If it's this hot with no sun, how will it feel during the day?* I remember thinking, *Never complain about the heat again.*

Another lasting impression was, later during training, it was so hot I had to wear gloves to hold my M-4 weapon so my hands wouldn't burn.

Two events happened in Kuwait at Camp Arifjan that affected me. First, while I was on convoy training, a local family was killed on a live-fire range. They were collecting brass for money. This event was classified as a training incident, but for me, it was the prelude to the disregard of non-American life I developed. It was like nothing happened. They shouldn't have been out there, was the attitude of everyone I was around.

Then training was shut down one day until command conducted an investigation. I never heard how the investigation ended, but we resumed training, back to business preparing for Iraq. In reflection, I frankly at the time didn't care about the family because I was focused on training and preparing for Iraq, but years later, I thought about that family.

The second event was running into Sergeant Bemore again, which seem to put me in my comfort zone with my deployment. I'd trained so much with him or been in the same unit with him over the years it made my deployment in the Middle East easier. He was someone I could relate to and talk with regarding my thoughts and concerns about the deployment.

In hindsight, I know being in a reserve unit, most soldiers get split up all over Iraq. As soon as you get familiar training with soldiers you didn't know, before long, you get attached to a different unit with new soldiers. I reflected back on my basic training days and what my drill sergeant said, "We're all green." I just reminded myself to focus on the mission! I'd completed all the training. Now, it was off to Iraq.

CHAPTER 12

IRAQ

Arriving in Iraq was very exciting to me, especially flying in over Baghdad, observing this large city below at night. I was excited. The mission was finally starting to feel real. Once I was on the ground, the view of the country was mind-blowing. There were no traffic lights. The streets were crowded like downtown K Street in DC at lunchtime on a summer day with a lot of people hanging out in front of shops and stores.

Eventually, I was inside the Green Zone, viewing government buildings and Saddam's beautiful palaces. It was cool. I thought about the rundown cramped housing I viewed while riding in the convoy into Baghdad city. I realized there were ghettos all over the world. I thought, *The haves and have-nots have no boundaries.*

I initially was housed in the Green Zone near Saddam's palace in a warehouse. I remember, on the side of the warehouse, there was a broken statue of Saddam's head. Some soldiers were taking pictures, but I wasn't tripping about it. Again, I was just focusing on the mission. Eventually, I settled in at night, ready for whatever. I was anxious with thoughts about completing this mission and getting back home.

In the morning, I reported to the first meeting. Then in a

matter of time, everything changed. I was reassigned to Camp Taji to the National Depot as a first sergeant. The mission was to train Iraqi counterparts and oversee the receiving and shipping out of equipment, uniforms, weapons, ammunition, and vehicles. I sat there stunned, wondering what happened with going to Al Kasick, which was in northern Iraq near Mosul.

I had prepared my mind to go up there into an isolated area. Then I quickly refocused, being flexible like my years in the army had taught me, especially as an infantry soldier and a drill sergeant.

After the meeting, I asked command why my assignment had changed. Command said that they felt I had the skills and experience to lead soldiers to accomplish the mission at Camp Taji, an important mission the Eightieth was responsible for. I took a deep breath and quickly went off by myself to pray. Then I told myself, "I'm ready."

Later that evening, I became apprehensive about working in a supply duty position that I hadn't done in many years. I second-guessed command's assignment. I felt a more logical assignment for me would be training Iraqi soldiers on a military transition team (MiTT) or being on a convoy team. Then I thought, *Military ain't about what you think is best for you. It is about what they think is best for the mission.*

Next, I reminded myself to stop overthinking and second-guessing command. I decided whatever my assignment focus, it is what is; the duty position would not change. I told myself, *Just be ready to roll with it, shorty. Do your thing, and go home.*

Finally, the next morning, we were rolling out on a convoy to Camp Taji. Stay alert, stay alive. It's action time.

CHAPTER 13

CAMP TAJI

I traveled from the Green Zone, Baghdad, to Taji on a convoy. I was anxious and hypervigilant from the beginning. I rode in an armored twelve-passenger bus with four Humvees providing protection and security. I remember feeling paranoid about not being able to protect myself inside a bus or having no control during the convoy. The only way I could fire or protect myself was if we dismounted from the vehicle, which we discussed in a safety briefing before departing. I felt helpless. I could only watch. I was not in control, especially when civilian cars tried to drive near or through our convoy. Those cars only stopped or moved out of way when Humvees fired warning shots. *Welcome to Iraq*, I thought.

Also, while riding to Taji, I observed people living on rooftops, in rundown houses, and on the roads; cows eating rubble; and people in long lines with containers for gas and water. Again, I was shocked at the poverty outside the Green Zone.

Finally arriving at Camp Taji, I was relieved and excited. I remember thinking, *Let's get this deployment over with.*

The first thing I noticed was that the base was divided in two: a US-Coalition side and an Iraqi side. Further, I saw the damage still evident from the 2003 bombings when US forces made the push into Iraq. There were a lot of destroyed tanks and warehouses at Camp Taji, a main Iraqi Army base.

My unit was housed on the Iraqi side, and the US-Coalition side was where Third Infantry Division and supporting units were housed to support the overall mission and security. There were checkpoints manned by Third Infantry Division within the base between the Coalition side and the Iraqi side. The depot was on the Iraqi side of the base. That day, I took a mental note of the lay of the land.

Only two members of my unit at the depot arrived with me. The rest of the soldiers would arrive in weekly intervals. Our housing was inside a warehouse with one-man trailers stacked up like an apartment building.

Let's Get It Started

The next morning, I met my counterpart first sergeant with whom I would cross-train to learn my responsibilities before he left the country in a week.

The commander was from another unit and was extending his tour; therefore, I would continue under this commander's leadership.

Immediately, I was thrown into action. The next night, weapons and ammunition were stolen out of the depot warehouses. The commander ordered all weapons and ammunition remaining to be moved closer to the front of the warehouses of the depot from the back of the depot, which was near the fence line toward the road to Taji.

The first sergeant's responsibility was organizing, motivating, and monitoring personnel to get it done. I worked side by side with the first sergeant, providing personnel assignments, security, and investigation of theft. We worked twenty-four hours, staying on site, observing soldiers moving ammunition and weapons with forklifts and then restacking them in new locations and securing warehouses by placing CONEX containers in front of them.

I realized immediately that danger lurked all around with the valuable equipment, weapons, and ammunition at Taji Depot. I became battle focused, quickly realizing there would always be a threat of attack.

Although I didn't know how to drive a forklift, it was clear my job as first sergeant was to organize, motivate, and maintain discipline while soldiers carried out the mission at the depot. Further, I had to take command of the theater of operations and ensure it was performed and carried out. I would be the buffer between command and soldiers.

During this first operation, safety became an issue at night. We couldn't use much light because of concern about mortar round attacks. For light, we used forklift and truck lights. Needless to say, vision was limited, and the threat of danger lurked all around.

The concern was an enemy attack and our soldiers getting hurt. At one point, soldiers began to complain about being out there at night and being tired from working all day. The first sergeant and I made up shifts, sending the majority of soldiers back to rest for four hours then to return, replacing the others. I remember the first sergeant and I taking alternating forty-five-minute naps after 2:00 a.m.

By the next morning, all the weapons and ammunition were moved and secured into warehouses. Then command made changes of personnel procedure for access to weapons and ammunition. Further, command reassigned the weapons and ammunition officer job to fall under the command of the Taji Depot's commanding officer.

I quickly realized how dangerous the Taji area was when mortar rounds started coming over the wall on the Iraqi side of the base where I slept. I also noticed how fast things could change in a war zone, along with how political it was in terms of who gets credit or blame with achieving the mission.

The soldiers from my unit, Eightieth Division, were arriving every week for the next three weeks until all were on the ground at Camp Taji, twenty-six in total.

The first thing I noticed that was unique about my soldiers was I had a majority of younger soldiers unlike the unit we were replacing. My initial thinking was having youth would be a strength, as they had more energy. My concern was that I didn't know and hadn't trained with any of the incoming Eightieth Division soldiers at Camp Atterbury. I felt rapport. Respect had to be established quickly, especially in a war zone, where you had to trust your fellow soldier to have your back.

At Camp Taji, I stayed in the first sergeant position for eight months. During that time, I cross-trained with the Iraqi Army and executed the daily mission. I experienced challenges with my US soldiers' adjustment to Iraq and performing their duties with Iraqi soldiers.

Several situations arose, which I handled, such as apprehension working with Iraqi soldiers and some becoming homesick or having relationship or family problems, but my US soldiers eventually adapted and adjusted, doing an outstanding job.

A situation occurred with one of my young soldiers at the depot who was having mental health problems adjusting to the Iraq War environment. He was eventually sent to Landstuhl, Germany, and then to Walter Reed Hospital in the United States for mental health support.

Later, during our deployment, we received the tragic news

that our young soldier died in an automobile accident, which sadly impacted everyone at the depot. For me specifically, I struggled with the news of his death. I remember thinking I didn't do enough to help my soldier and blaming myself for his death.

Also, I developed agitation with daily meetings with our Iraqi Army counterparts and an interpreter translating for both during our afteraction evening meetings. For eight months, the frustration was with what was being said being translated correctly and the length of meetings up to sixty minutes daily. Also, I had agitation with Iraqi soldiers leaving every week. We trained Iraqi soldiers and then had to do it all over again with new soldiers. I was thinking there was no accountability for Iraqis, but US soldiers were expected to be robots and carry out the mission with or without the Iraqi soldiers' support.

Further, I was frustrated with my unit being assigned additional duty guarding the south gate of Taji, where Iraqi soldiers and contractors entered the base. One serious situation occurred at the south gate, a VBIED attack that killed twelve and wounded six Iraqi soldiers and civilians. I remember thinking, *Thank God none of my soldiers were down there, and there were no US-Coalition hurt.*

I will never forget that day because I was driving to the south gate area when it happened, and it was the loudest sound I had ever heard. The ground was shaking. I remember seeing the aftermath hole in the ground, car pieces, blood, and body parts. It's an image I'll always remember.

Another situation that caused some duty stress was my unit providing transportation to the south gate for our Iraqi depot soldiers to vote off base and then return back to Taji Depot. I remember command giving a safety warning about soldiers wearing suicide vests returning; however, nothing happened.

Everyone was hypervigilant and alert that day, bracing for something to happen. Thank God nothing did.

I had a close call with a mortar round (Katyusha) landing fifty meters from me at the depot. That day, I supervised my US soldiers and Iraqi soldiers off-loading trucks that had arrived at Taji for the Iraqi Army. During the off-loading, I remember noticing about a hundred meters away an Iraqi soldier who appeared to have a cell phone walking away from the off-loading ramp.

I was suspicious because the Iraqi soldiers at the depot were not allowed to have weapons or cell phones. When I walked over to the Iraqi soldier with my interperter, the soldier said he didn't have a phone and walked away. I didn't think about it anymore, refocusing on safety with off-loading the trucks.

After all the trucks were off-loaded and parked at the depot. I went to double-check CONEX containers near the off-loading ramp to ensure they were secured. All of sudden, I heard a whistling sound. I hit the ground and then *boom*. I got up dazed with ears ringing and then checked myself. I looked up and saw the mortar round had hit where the trucks were off-loaded. I quickly thanked God for not being hurt. Then I realized if it had been thirty minutes earlier, soldiers would have been in that spot. Now I thought that Iraqi soldier did have a phone and was calling that mortar round in. Damn!

Meanwhile, command was still pressuring me about putting in the E-8 promotion packet. I continued to resist. I remember feeling the growing tension with command regarding having an E-7 in an E-8 position, especially with how I forcefully communicated my thoughts about the mission.

In March 2006, my duty assignment was changed to an E-7 position after another theft of weapons from Taji Depot. I suspected an Iraqi contractor of the thefts and confronted him. I was verbally reprimanded by command about my confrontation with this Iraqi contractor.

One week later, I was being transferred to the outpost Camp Buckmaster in Tikrit, Iraq. I felt politically I had offended the Iraqi contractor and command was tired of an E-7 being in an E-8 position; therefore, command removed me. I only became more agitated and frustrated with the lack of follow-up about the contractor's involvement with the theft of weapons and ammunition.

I was all right with my job and post change; however, my worries arose with how difficult it was to travel to Camp Buckmaster. Convoy travel was not authorized because of high IED threat on the road and enemy small-arms fire. I remember my convoy being cancelled twice because of road security danger for personnel travel.

Eventually, I traveled to Camp Buckmaster by helicopter with two Iraqi officers, making an awkward trip with no words spoken. We just stared at one another. However, it was exciting flying by helicopter, and I enjoyed the view of the country from above. I arrived safely to Buckmaster and prepared for this assignment, relieved at not being responsible for other soldiers but only myself.

My frustration arose the next week when those Iraqi officers mysteriously were gone, and command said they were not sending any more Iraqi officers up there. I was frustrated with the difference between the US and Iraqi Armies. It was one minute here, next week gone, and then the same thing happened again, while US soldiers stayed in place and carried out a mission. Ugh!

Camp Buckmaster's composition was predominately contractors on post and one Eightieth Division soldier there with me. Our job was monitoring and reporting weapons and ammunition being received and shipped out to command in the Green Zone or other parts of Iraq.

Also, Camp Buckmaster was a hasty collection point for captured enemy weapons. Our additional duty was monitoring civilian Iraqis who loaded and off-loaded weapons and ammunition with US contractors.

I got adjusted and established good rapport with my fellow Eightieth Division E-7 soldier. The difficult part was being in an isolated outpost, leaving a heavily populated secured Camp Taji with American soldiers.

It was like being incarcerated, never leaving the outpost and being wary of civilian Iraqis. There was a constant threat of attack because of the weapons and ammunitions on base without US military support. The nearest support was Camp Remagen Air Base.

Another situation that had me hypervigilant and anxious was contractors provided camp security. The security force was from Fiji Island. I slept in a one-man trailer locked and loaded with my M-4 and nine millimeter in my bed, paranoid because I lacked confidence in camp security. I remember thinking our campsite would be overrun by insurgents.

Eventually, I adjusted to Camp Buckmaster, and time went by fast. My fifteen-day leave was scheduled in May. I was looking forward to it just to leave Camp Buckmaster and see other people, along with better eating in the Green Zone chow hall, and then to get home to see my family and friends.

CHAPTER 14

FIFTEEN-DAY LEAVE

While time was getting close for my fifteen-day leave, I thought how I had modeled selfless service while at Camp Taji. I scheduled my fifteen-day leave after all my soldiers at Taji Depot went home before me. I learned and applied selfless service like my basic training drill sergeant taught me twenty-three years ago.

I became agitated when the problem with transportation out of Camp Buckmaster outpost became an issue. The problem was getting back to the Green Zone to fly out of the country. One option was getting to Camp Remagen to board helicopter services to fly back to the Green Zone in Baghdad. I asked command why helicopters couldn't come to Camp Buckmaster like when I arrived. I remember being told that was not happening for one soldier.

My dilemma was no convoy would transport one soldier, which was me, to Camp Remagen due to safety of personnel. I remember thinking about the Johnny Guitar Watson song, "Ain't That a Bitch," upset with how I would get back to Baghdad for my leave.

Someone made the suggestion to ride in a civilian convoy to return to the Green Zone in Baghdad. A civilian convoy would be coming through Camp Buckmaster and going to Baghdad. My command was aware of my travel plan, and I had to sign a waiver to ride with a civilian contractor convoy.

During the civilian convoy to Baghdad, we were shot at with small-arms fire multiple times and pulled off the road because of reported IEDs. Then the army emergency response team had to clear the road for us to continue the convoy. It seemed like an eternity with a two-hour ride becoming a four-hour ride to Camp Liberty outside Baghdad.

Then the next day, I rode in a civilian convoy from Camp Liberty to the Baghdad Green Zone. While on that convoy, we rode past trucks damaged and civilians injured by an IED attack on highway Irish a couple of hours ahead of us.

I was frustrated with the civilian convoy experience and lack of support to get back to Baghdad by my command. Once in the Green Zone, I almost didn't go home. I was upset and concerned how I would feel when I got home. However, I knew my family wanted to see me, and it would disappoint them if I didn't come home.

I reluctantly went home, fighting off thoughts that when I got home, I would stay. I became upset thinking that then I just wanted this tour to be over with. I was thinking August was not far away; then the tour would be over. Also, I remembered feeling that by going home, I would be jinxing myself. I thought when I returned to Iraq, I would get killed. I thought about the song by the rap group Ghetto Boys, "My Mind Playing Tricks on Me." I was tripping singing one verse daily as a joke: "I keep peeping around corners feeling like a goner, my mind playing tricks on me."

Then I thought about how, once home, I'd get a couple of drinks and everything would be good. I didn't realize how drinking alcohol was my coping mechanism at the time. I just decided to go home. It would be good for me to see my family.

I returned to US soil happy and excited to see my family and friends; however, I became anxious and hypervigilant immediately while riding home from the airport in traffic, thinking about my convoy experiences.

Further, I easily became frustrated, having inner conflict and being inappropriate in communicating with family and friends. For nine months, I'd been yelling and cussing nonstop in Iraq: "Mf this, Mf that, shit, God damn" came spitting out my mouth daily. I thought, *Lord, help me!*

In hindsight, I was uncomfortable the whole time home, oddly missing being in Iraq with my soldiers. Then, the next minute, I'd be mad that I had waited so long to go on leave, noticing the changes within my marriage, children, and job.

Another situation had me nervous and conflicted, and that was returning to visit the high school where I coached boys' basketball. On reflection, I can see this visit impacted me the most while on leave because I lost something I valued because of being deployed.

Visiting the school, I was feeling nervous about seeing the students. How would they respond seeing me, and how would I react? I debated in my mind just not visiting the school and going back home. Then I thought I would jinx myself and get killed if I did visit. I felt crazy guilty, like I wanted to see them because if I didn't, I would feel terrible—the old damned if you do, damned if you don't situation was playing out in my mind.

During my visit, I found out I wouldn't return as boys' varsity coach the next season. I was shocked not to be the coach upon my return. I was stunned, and my initial thought was *This is not that hero welcome I envisioned. Wow!*

I walked into the hallway and spoke briefly with students

and staff while trying to leave and fighting back tears. I put on my game face and hugged a few students quickly before walking to the door to leave. Once outside, I was walking back to my vehicle, and tears welled up in my eyes, but nothing rolled down my face. I got inside my car and just sped off in disbelief at the news I'd received.

After driving a couple of blocks, I pulled over, wondering how this could happen. I missed the season because of being deployed to Iraq. There had been no mention made about any coaching changes after school ended before my deployment. What was happening?

I got myself together before returning home and became battle focused with returning to Iraq in a few days. My army training as an infantry soldier kicked in, and I remembered how I was taught men dealt with shit. You channeled your emotions. The old army mantra, "Suck it up, soldier," came to mind. I thought, *Just continue to march. The tour's almost over. You can deal with it.*

When I told my family and friends that I would not be coaching basketball next season, everybody was shocked and upset, feeling I was being mistreated, especially being told this before having to go back to Iraq. I was getting more upset after their reactions.

I reasoned with everyone, while psyching myself up with being thankful for not being hurt or dead. Then I asked everybody to stop talking about it and let`me focus on completing my mission in Iraq. The next day, I remember not wanting to talk about it anymore, suppressing my feelings and then drinking a six-pack alone to numb my feelings.

I got into my drill sergeant mode quickly while flying back to Iraq. I was thinking, *Be battle-focused. Mission first. I'll defend shit.* All the while, I was crushed emotionally and having to push those feelings deep down to focus on my return to Iraq.

While returning to Iraq on the plane, I reflected how I was fighting for the country and the school system and other people didn't seem to appreciate my sacrifice and services. I thought about the saying, "Outta sight, outta mind." I was thinking that I had been the assistant coach of the city championship and number-one-ranked team in DC area. Also, two years as the head coach meant nothing to this high school administration. Wow, I was in total disbelief at this cruel twist of fate with my community and professional life.

I allowed negative thoughts to rush my mind while on the flight back to Iraq, until after someone told the flight attendant, "Give that soldier any drink he wants while on this flight." I had three Heineken beers, thank you very much! I was finally appreciated, I thought. "Burp."

While I reflect back to this moment, I see that a negative seed was planted inside me during my fifteen-day leave. I believed God was turning his back on me. Wow, welcome home, Soldier!

Here I Am, Listen to the Invisible Man Poem

I'm a Black Iraq veteran, returning citizen now
I feel trap no hood, no job, VA not giving me
what I earned just like 40 acres and a mule, feel
like a fool

God gives me hope, reality makes me mad,
adversity makes me strong, common sense say
don't do wrong! DC invisible man moving on,
seem only my family and friends see me now.

I can't hold a job, difficulty working due to my PTSD. Realizing I made it hard by making illegal choices, but now frustrated watching my community changing before my eyes. I'm not saying it's bad or good, but damn I miss my hood!

I feel alone, then that invisible spirit power of God touches my soul. I got strength now to go on, wait, be quiet "sshh." Invisible man making moves, trying to share, help the next man, woman, vet, and returning citizen with thoughts to refocus.

Hocus pocus here I am, man with wisdom, knowledge, and experiences willing to share. Look at me! Validated by God realizing my power, knowing he always my friend in my darkest hour; I push on. Do you hear my voice? I'm your conscious. Look at me! I'm your man, father, brother, friend, Matter of Time at it again!

Yelling to the world, Don't lock me out! You will acknowledge and respect me! Try and hold me back because of a felony, feel like jealousy! I'm free, black, strong, knowing I belong!

I learned to channel my emotions and reaction by writing this poem. I remembered Chuck D of Public Enemy saying, "When you get mad, put it down on a pad, give you something you never had!"

It's good now being legal and productive, praying these words to heal and inspire, helping you to reach higher!

Now in a matter of time, learn how to get stress off your mind. Get yours, while I get mine, so you won't be left behind! January 2013 supervised release

ANGER

My Iraq transition caused me anger. *Webster's* definition of *anger* is a "hostile feeling or wrath".

I learned in PTSD treatment that everyone experiences anger. It is not a bad feeling but a normal and healthy one; however, your actions and response determine if it is healthy or detrimental to you and your relationships.

Webster's definition of *resentment* is the feeling of displeasure "at an act, remark, person, or so on regarded as causing injury or insult".

Resentment is anger's brother and develops from anger. Resentment is the way most of us react to our past experiences that make us angry. It can hinder a person's growth by making him or her relive past experiences again and again in the mind, therefore remaining angry.

My approach of coping with anger when I returned home from Iraq caused me to crash socially. I began to isolate myself and self-medicate with alcohol. I became easily agitated. Then the anger developed into resentment about my deployment, causing me inner turmoil.

Anger during my transition home was fueled by my perception of going to Iraq and leaving my family and job willingly to defend and protect my country. However, I felt my experiences transitioning home were not respected by society's actions toward me.

In treatment, I identified things that made me angry, eventually turning into resentment during my transition from Iraq. They include

- losing my coaching job, which was important to me
- not being acknowledged by my employer or even welcomed home the next school year
- having no party or acknowledgment in formation but only a flag sent in the mail when I retired from the army reserve

I believe it's important to respect and honor soldiers! Also, the initial services I received from the VA hospital caused me turmoil. I remember having issues with counseling and medication.

I had difficulty with expressing myself with staff at the VA hospital. I felt a lack of cultural understanding hindered me in accepting help.

Also, I felt pushed onto medication and had difficulty finding the right dosage. I reported side effects only to be given another pill. It made me feel like I had to drug up just to cope. I then rationalized, why not self-medicate with alcohol? I was told, "You're being noncompliant with treatment." Ugh!

Those first couple of years, I became angrier and more frustrated with everybody and everything. My understanding was Mr. Johnnie Walker Scotch got me. This eventually was a bad coping strategy for me, costing my mental health and freedom.

Not dealing with my anger in a positive manner caused major resentment in me, and it impacted my view on life and professional relationships. I felt paranoid, thinking people looked at me in awe because of my services over in Iraq but were saying, "He's another crazy veteran beneath the surface."

My anger made me unable to describe my feelings and thoughts effectively to family, and I had difficulty with continuing some relationships with friends. Therefore, I became lonely and depressed.

During my attempts at treatment, once they learned of my occupation as a social worker, I often received statements like "You should understand" or "You know how to respond in a positive manner," which only made me angry and feel stupid. I eventually stopped participating or even going to treatment.

Now in hindsight, I understand anger and resentment caused havoc in my life, mentally and emotionally. Further, I noticed how anger shows your character defects and shortcomings, but if dealt with properly, it can build up your personal strength. I eventually found my strength in, of all places, prison.

Through my heartache and pain, I realized the importance of developing an approach, technique, and methodology to cope with anger.

My first step was honestly being able to acknowledge alcohol and PTSD as problems in my life. I encourage you to be honest with yourself, and whatever issue impacts you negatively, have hope and faith and develop a positive approach, technique, and methodology to overcome your trials and difficulties in life. Find one, and apply it!

Also, if you are consistent with treatment and determined, you can overcome life's obstacles. If you open your eyes, there are examples of God's blessings around or in your life. I can remember examples from coaching and being a drill sergeant that showed me consistent practice, training, and determination can bring positive results.

Further, I suggest you explore and enhance your spirituality. You might develop faith that God's grace and mercy will help you overcome whatever you're up against in a *matter of time*!

CHAPTER 15

MY JOURNEY WITH TREATMENT

When I returned home from Iraq in August 2006, I was confused about my war experiences and had difficulty managing my thoughts and emotions. I realized I would need mental health treatment after a couple of months home because of the difficulty sleeping, nightmares, anxiety in crowded situations, agitation, and anger all the time. Therefore, I humbled myself and sought help.

I first went to the vet center for help. I went through the intake interview and was referred to the veterans hospital for a physical and further mental health evaluation. I was assigned to a treatment team who would manage my physical and mental health needs.

After assessment, I was diagnosed with PTSD and depression, titintus and was immediately prescribed medication. I was not a person who usually got sick or took medication prior to this deployment, so it was a big adjustment for me.

I reluctantly took medication, hoping how I felt and interacted with others would improve immediately by taking these damn pills. Throughout these past years, I had found out getting improvement from PTSD by medication alone does not work.

I returned home angry (emotion), which made me have a strong desire to drink (feel), which caused me to become depressed and frustrated with my situation. I realize now I was in "denial" (*didn't even [k]now I am lying*) about my condition.

My initial experience and reaction to receiving medication was conflicted because I felt like medication was pushed on me before any other actions were taken. You can't sleep—a pill. You're mad—a pill. You feel sad—a pill. *Damn! Give me something else besides a pill!* I thought. Years later, I was introduced to alternative treatment, such as meditation, acupuncture, and yoga.

Further frustration with treatment came at being told, "Don't drink alcohol," which I had done the majority of my life, especially while on military duty and therefore found hard to stop. This made me angrier with the hypocrisy, because you want me to use your drugs but not my drug of choice? Liquor! I tried to comply by abstaining from alcohol for a few weeks, and then the prescribed medication made me sick.

I attempted to find out why side effects with medicine were happening and maybe consider new medicine. However, at the time, the VA process to see a psychiatrist (three to four months) was lengthy, and if you went to the emergency room, you had a long wait and then the questions: "Do you feel like harming yourself or others?" I wanted to say, "I feel like hurting you, damn it!"

Because of these self-perceived barriers, I stopped taking the medication and going to services. I began to self-medicate with alcohol, with which I felt instant relief. I enjoyed self-medicating more than prescribed medication usage. In hindsight, I was masking more problems, and I was in complete denial of my situation.

After a year, my attitude changed about medication at times.

I intermittently took prescribed meds and still self-medicated; however, I never found the right medication dosage. For me, this caused conflicting thoughts and actions with taking prescribed medication.

Now, my real frustration with trying to receive treatment was again coping with "Oh, you're a social worker. You understand how to get better." It seemed everybody assumed I could recover from PTSD and depression. *Nobody listened to me*!

Any service provider should take this suggestion: be nonjudgmental; listen to your client's or patient's thoughts and concerns; and then allow input with the treatment method as long as safety is not compromised.

Also, I was frustrated with using medication. Eventually, I rejected VA services and treatment, developing my own treatment plan in 2007. My plan was to stay busy returning to coaching, working with youth in a part-time capacity at my old Boys and Girls Club while continuing full time as a special education social worker. My goal was to simulate the long work hours and that adrenaline rush like I had in Iraq.

However, this plan impacted my interactions with family negatively as far as quality time spent. Selfishly, I felt that rush of excitement through feeling I could get better on my own. I thought, *Yeah, I'm rocking steady again*, like that Whispers' eighties song.

I walked a tightrope for four years, struggling to maintain my responsibility at home and professionally while coping with PTSD. Unfortunately, I was heading for a collision with not consistently being in treatment or on medication. It felt like each year, more problems were building up. I responded with poor coping skills and then the finger-pointing at others with no personal accountability. Then I finally turned to drinking liquor to mask and cope with it all.

I remember fighting with my military training thoughts of *Drive on*, and *Infantry always move forward*. My community training brought this thought: *Handle your business*. Therefore, I never took inventory of my thoughts and feelings and how they were impacting me. I pushed it all inside myself. My outlet again was alcohol.

Later on, during my journey through and after incarceration, I accepted the concept of receiving treatment. I realized the lack of treatment in my community led me to jail.

While incarcerated, I briefly began taking medication again at night so it would help me sleep and improve my agitated mood; however, I was groggy and sluggish in the morning. It was difficult to continue medication usage while incarcerated because seeing a doctor and receiving good care, such as an explanation of side effects, was not easy.

I remember thinking the reality was that my mental health needs were of no concern to staff. The staff was there for eight hours—just take the meds and don't cause any problems around them. After a month of medication usage, not liking the side effects, like drowsiness in the morning lasting to around ten, I stopped, cold turkey.

I felt medication usage was not helping my emotions or feelings while I was locked up. Ironically, I found hope in God's word and believing God would heal me.

Now, two programs that made a difference while I was incarcerated were anger management and the Twelve-Step Alcohol/Drug program at CTF jail. While participating in a group and restoring my relationship with God, I was able to see how much influence alcohol had over my life.

I thought maybe if I restored my relationship with God by reading the Bible daily and going to Bible study / church services, I could improve. In addition, I exercised daily, getting that stress relief and adrenaline rush. I began to believe clearly whatever does not begin with God will end in failure. It was then I decided to recommit my walk with God, regardless of my circumstances or situation.

While participating in group and restoring my relationship with God, I was able to see how much influence alcohol had over my life. I interacted with others, celebrating promotions, a job well done, and victory in all social situations, it seemed. When I was coping with deaths and disappointments, using alcohol was the norm too.

Also, I thought of my past experiences of car crashes and DUI arrests. I rationalized those situations away. I did not see the dangers because no one got hurt or I escaped with no consequences. Now, with my freedom gone, I was facing the reality that alcohol brought me here.

Reflecting on my experiences of PTSD treatment, I believe medication only for anxiety or mood problems is not the end-all answer. I found improvement with combining medication, spirituality, and group or individual counseling with a focus on anger management, safety, decision making, and self-control skills. In my humble opinion, this should be implemented for treatment with veterans and returning citizens.

In addition, I believe in applying this basic saying to those in treatment, "Control what you can control—*you*!"

CHAPTER 16

I SNAPPED!

It was 2010, four years after transitioning from Iraq. During those four years, I walked a tightrope, unable to balance my life with family, work, the deaths of former players and mentors, and coping with PTSD.

The most impactful situation affecting me was watching my father's health deteriorating. He twice was in and out of the hospital and then the nursing home for rehabilitation. Also, my DC school job was becoming more stressful with new evaluation procedures and the shift of decreasing union influence with personnel matters.

In addition, I had concerns regarding all four of my children being productive in their lives and how I could assist. Plus, I worried about my grandchildren's development and progress in school.

I remember thinking additional money could reduce some of my stress, so I decided to apply for a $20,000 loan at my military credit union. I believed approval would easily be made. I was a war veteran from Iraq paying my bills. However, I was denied the loan due to my old cell phone bill I accrued while over Iraq. Before departing to Iraq, I had requested cell phone services be turned off. I never read the fine print requiring me to pay until the contract expired. This made me furious. I had to provide proof of being in Iraq, and that required me to express myself calmly, which I had difficulty doing. It took two months before I got this matter corrected. I became very frustrated with this taking so long because of my inability to communicate without yelling and cussing on the phone. Eventually, I resolved this matter by paying two months before my deployment to Iraq; the rest of the bill was waived.

I resubmitted for the personal loan only to be denied again; however, I was approved for a home equity loan, which I didn't want to do.

I was heated like a well-lit fireplace. I was full of anger, feeling like a victim at not being respected as a veteran again, especially with my loan not being approved. Then the "Why me?" attacked every night. I would lie awake, replaying my Iraq experiences and difficulty with the transition home. I felt like my back was against the wall and nobody understood or cared about my service for this country or community.

During all this, I kept things to myself, seeking relief with continued drinking after work and checking on my father. My only joy was returning to coach high school basketball again as an assistant coach. Coaching provided a distraction from negative thoughts, and it gave me that army camaraderie feeling again.

Now, the log that made the fire hotter was my truck was repossessed one Monday morning because I was two months late in payment. I was in denial of my irresponsible action with not paying on time or not making late payment arrangements. I only had seven months to pay off the damn truck, but my sick mind felt there would be no problem with paying late. Further, my plan was to pay two months' on my next payday that upcoming Friday.

Ironically, I called the week before my payday to make arrangements. In my inability to control my anger, I cussed out the representative who I perceived was disrespectful to me. I didn't think much more about it, knowing I would pay two months' on payday.

My thinking then was I had paid late before many times since returning from Iraq. I never thought the snatch man would get me. I awoke one morning to a tow truck driver blocking my garage and threatening to call the police if I didn't allow him to tow my truck, which was inside my garage. We briefly argued. I stepped back inside the house, saying, "Be there when I come back." He ran to his truck again, threatening to call the police.

Inside the house, my family was asking what was going on. I stopped going to get my house protector, suddenly feeling embarrassed by the situation. I reluctantly opened the garage and then watched my truck get towed away, seething hot.

I contacted the lender, and they said if I didn't pay within fifteen days, they were going to sell my car. I was livid thinking of all the money I had spent on the truck. I was like, *Now they want to take it when it's almost paid off?* still never taking any responsibility for not paying on time. Now I had to pay two months' bills, towing, and storage.

My PTSD was in full force. I was stressing about my father being in the nursing home and having no car. I felt like an animal backed into a corner, ready to fight back. I was feeling the weight of a terrible four-year transition from Iraq. At my lowest point, I was feeling like a disrespected veteran.

Responding to this current car crisis, I had to juggle transportation, sharing a car with my significant other until Friday when I got paid. My pride stopped me from asking anybody for help. I was embarrassed and furious about this situation. I felt nobody could help me. My anxiety and agitation went to new heights with having to share a car for a few days too. Each day without my truck, I felt like a failure.

I was frustrated at my new travel schedule with one car. It disrupted how I drove my mother daily to visit my father at the nursing home, especially without my truck. I dreaded the thought of her asking, "Where is your truck at?"

One morning en route to work, I was stuck in standstill traffic because of a car accident. While stuck in traffic, I felt hopeless, like a failure because I didn't have the money to get my truck until Friday. I was thinking about the storage fee being added daily, becoming even more upset. I felt like a failure.

Also, while stuck in traffic, I knew this routine wasn't going to work with sharing one car. Again, because of my pride, I didn't want to ask anybody for any money and was becoming impatient with waiting until Friday for payday.

All of a sudden, the frustration and agitation that had been building up during my four-year transition just boiled over, like a hot tea pot whistling. I screamed, cried, and banged the steering wheel. I remember the person in the car beside me looking over at me like I was crazy. I yelled and cussed, "Stop looking at me!" Reflecting back, I can see this was the most agitated anger I had felt about everything since returning home. My head felt like it was going to explode.

Eventually, I arrived at work late and sat in the parking lot, deciding if I should go inside the school to work. I was concerned about my mental state and feeling I had no patience that day to deal with students or adults. I remember thinking, *I'm gonna hit one of those kids or staff if they tripping today*. I decided to call in, saying, "I'm not able to work today." I drove off in a rage, not caring about using the little leave I had left.

I eventually got myself together and picked my mother

up to visit my father early. During the visit, I was quiet. My mother and father kept asking me if I was all right, and I replied, "Everything is okay," never mentioning my truck was repossessed or that I needed assistance with money. After the visit, I dropped my mother back home, and then I drove around thinking.

While I was driving, my mind went to how they had snatched my car and I wasn't approved for a personal loan. *With all I had sacrificed in the military and for my community, now look how I'm treated.*

Then I made a hasty action plan, thinking I would show "them" by robbing a bank. I reconned several banks, surveyed escape routes, and considered my approach and traffic patterns.

Then I made a big decision whether to take a gun or pass a note. I knew if I took a gun, I would use it if anybody got in my way. Then for a moment, I thought about just killing myself. Everything would be over—no bills, no worries.

The rest of the day, my mind and heart were swirling like a tornado with thoughts of robbing a bank or killing myself. I decided to rob the bank! I wanted to live! I thought about my family and how much hurt would be on them if I did that.

My thoughts that evening were about executing the bank robbery the next day. I went back out to recon the bank area again, utilizing my infantry skills.

That night, I lay awake, anxious, thinking about my approach to the bank teller, debating again if I should take my gun. I thought, *Just sleep on it, and decide in the morning.*

The next morning, I was excited and nervous about my plan to rob the bank. I called in sick to my job. While I was driving to the bank, it seemed like that Iraq feeling was coming back. Strangely, I felt alive with a purpose. On reflection, I see my moral compass was broken. I wasn't thinking about consequences and how I could hurt my family.

Once at the bank, I contemplated my approach. Deciding on no gun, I left it in the car. I thought to blend in with no mask to alert anybody of a robbery. My plan was to walk in, just hand a note to the teller, get money, put the money into a bag, walk out, and disappear. I didn't care if cameras saw me, thinking nobody had noticed me anyway since I'd been home.

While walking into the bank, I remember taking a deep breath and thinking, *Do it. You're only taking what you're owed.* I waited in line, approached the teller, handed over the note, got the money, put it in the bag, walked out, and blended in. Then I disappeared. Driving away, I thought, *Mission accomplished.* Later, I was counting the money, $6,700, thinking I had more than enough to get my truck the next day. I then felt a sick sense of accomplishment and excitement at robbing the bank.

Later that evening, I had conflicting thoughts about my criminal actions, feeling remorseful and thinking my family would be disappointed in me. However, I felt that rush at creating a plan and executing it without a hitch! While counting the money again, I felt good, thinking, *Now you getting back what is owed to you.*

The next day, I got my truck back. I felt vindicated against the banks and everybody who showed me no respect since returning from Iraq.

Then a life changer happened the next week: my father died. I was crushed, feeling my actions caused my father to die early, even though he had been sick the last two years. I repressed my feelings again and assisted my mother with funeral arrangements. Then I used some bank robbery money to pay for programs, food, and new suits for me and my sons.

In the days leading up to the funeral, I thought about how

the one person on earth who had my back was gone, which made me even more depressed. I pretended around people that I was okay. In hindsight, I know I was faking, thinking, *I can handle it. I'm good.* However, I was really distraught at the death of my father.

My cousins from Atlanta came to town, and I found comfort and peace of mind with their presence, like always. Also, my cousins from Indianapolis on my mother's side of the family came for support too.

A couple of days after the funeral, I felt like my whole world was gone without my dad. I had anger about my criminal actions and pain about my difficult transition home. It was like I cared, but I didn't care. I was unable to express my feelings to family or friends. I kept things to myself, finding relief only through alcohol, Johnnie Walker Black Scotch. I was living a double life as a father, social worker, coach, alcoholic, and bank robber.

Mr. Johnnie Walker Scotch convinced me to repeat this bank robbery behavior for the next five months, seeking that Iraq rush and getting back at society, in my mind, for not caring about me regarding my service to the country and community. I felt like the music group War's song: I was "slippin' into darkness."

CHAPTER 17

REFLECTIONS ABOUT PTSD

Post-traumatic stress disorder has had a major impact on most soldiers who served in combat zones and is now recognized for treatment. During the Iraq and Afghanistan Wars and operations, the reservists and national guardsmen have been heavily involved and used.

The Department of Veterans Affairs says more than 200,000 combat veterans (16 percent of the 1.3 million who fought) have been treated for PTSD since the Afghanistan and Iraq Wars began. When the invasion turned into an occupation, the Pentagon grew heavily dependent on reservists and national guardsmen with specialized expertise—business executives, lawyers, police officers, social workers, psychologists, and the like—to try to build the institutions of a new Iraqi society. A heavy family, physical, and mental health price has been paid by reservists and guardsmen.(USA TODAY, 2011)

Reintegration from wartime to home life from deployment has crushed many families. Three million Americans have had a spouse or parent deployed since 9/11, many multiple times, says Paul Riechoff, founder and executive director of the Advocacy Group Iraq and Afghanistan Veterans of America. (USA TODAY, 2011)

Therefore, experts know that soldiers' re-entry home is full of hidden hazards, which they have seen played out over and over again in the many years US troops have been deployed.

I point out active-duty soldiers return to military bases with medical care and networks that try to assist in reintegration home to family and society. Reservists do not have access to the same systems or networks and live without the psychological safety net that comes from living near and seeing members of their unit daily. National guardsmen and reservists suffer high rates of PTSD, alcoholism, unemployment, divorce, and drug abuse.

I was reading all this information from the newspapers and magazines while incarcerated in federal prison. I thought, *Damn, look at all the damage PTSD has caused to others, not just to me.*

I reflected on how my reserve unit's division was reorganized at the end of my deployment. I was due to retire in two months, and my unit allowed me not to go to drill with excused absences. I was realizing how those circumstances made me fall through the cracks. Nobody checked on how I was doing with transitioning back home. I had no retirement party, only a flag sent in the mail.

My transition from Iraq consisted of hurt, frustration, anger, and resentment, which grew inside daily like planted grass seeds growing in the spring.

CHAPTER 18

MY ARREST

It was a rainy day in August 2010, the second day back for the new school year. I was in school training when I received a telephone call that the police were at my home looking for me.

The police needed to talk with me ASAP and wanted to know my whereabouts. I stated, "I'll be there in about twenty minutes."

Rushing home, I immediately knew what they were there for, the bank robberies. While I was driving home, many thoughts were in my mind about my father, my tour of duty in Iraq, my rough transition home, and how my family, friends, current and former players, clients, and students would feel about all this. I remember thinking, *Just when I decided to stop, they got me. Damn, I'm caught.*

Then my mind replayed the day before. I had noticed a man in a car following me to my street, but he kept going, and then then later that evening, I got pulled over by police for a traffic stop. He gave me a warning ticket but insisted on taking my picture, talking about some area drug task force. If I refused, he would arrest me. I reluctantly consented, not wanting to be arrested, thinking I would file a complaint later about this harassment.

Once home, I was arrested and then transported to the police station. At the station, I was handcuffed to a table in an interview room and read my rights. I waived my right to a lawyer so they could hurry up and question me.

I was shown surveillance pictures of me in the bank and the clothing they had found in one area of the bank that matched the bank photos. I just looked at everything, saying nothing about what they showed me. The detective insisted I respond to these pictures he was showing me. I didn't respond because of how I was being talked to, all rough and disrespectful.

Another detective came into the room. He stated he knew I was a retired army veteran, and he hoped things would work out, but now it was over. I recognized him as the man who had been following me the day before. Then he showed me photos from the last bank I'd robbed in another county. He paused and then showed me a picture of my truck leaving the parking garage where I had parked. The picture showed my shirt and arm visible but not my face. He had my attention.

The detective stated my shirt matched the bank photo, and he used my truck tag number to look up my driver's license. He said my photo resembled the bank photo. Then he got my address.

I was thinking back on how on that robbery, I got my first dye pack and heard sirens. I didn't get a chance to take off my shirt like I usually did. Plus, I remembered how I couldn't let the window up because of the dye pack smoke.

The detective stood up, put the pictures back inside the folder, and said, "That is how I got a lead to find you for questioning." He stated one county was going to charge me for the five banks I'd robbed there and another county would charge me for the one I did there. While leaving the room, he turned back and said, "I don't think you're a bad man." He said he understood tough times and that he was a veteran too. He added, "But do the right thing, confess."

Reality hit me. I was caught! Oddly enough, the Grandmaster Flash and the Furious Five Song "The Message" went through my mind, especially one verse, "Don't push me. I'm close to the edge. I'm trying not to lose my head." I was thinking, *Damn, my freedom gone and probably be locked up for years.* Later, I admitted my guilt, trying to slow down the rushing thoughts in my head.

I was processed, fingerprinted, swabbed for a DNA sample, and pictured. I was then transported to jail. While riding to jail again, I heard the song lyrics, "Don't push me. I'm close to the edge. I'm trying not to lose my head." I thought, *Too late now, I'm losing my freedom too. Wow!*

Later on, upon consultation with a lawyer, I was told it would be better to be charged federally so all six bank robberies could be combined instead of split up between the two counties. I was told even though there was only one charge in one county, they were not going to give it to the county with the most charges; therefore, I would have to serve whatever my sentence was for both counties. I felt overwhelmed, thinking, *What a mess! It seems like some slave shit I put myself in.*

I eventually got out on bail bond. I quickly resigned from my job and tried to prepare my family for my incarceration, asking forgiveness for my actions and exploring my legal options.

Then one morning, the US Marshalls stormed my house and arrested me, and I was charged for the bank robberies in federal court. I remember thinking I wouldn't be free for years now.

My arrest experiences had me feeling ashamed, embarrassed, and unsure of my future.

CHAPTER 19

JAIL EXPERIENCE

> For our light affliction which is but for a moment, worketh for us a far more exceeding and eternal weight of glory.
>
> —2 Corinthians 4:17 (KJ21)

I spent four days in one county jail before making bond; however, the other county arrested me for their bank robbery arrest warrant. I spent three days in that county jail before making bail again.

I was held in federal custody at CTF Jail in DC, where I remained for ten months until my sentencing.

While in jail awaiting sentencing, I was unsure about my future. I started to read the Bible daily, attended Bible services when available, and fellowshipped with other inmates having Bible study. Some people call this "jailhouse religion." Now you're in trouble, so you turn to God to get your sentence reduced or get found not guilty. For me, it was real. Losing my freedom and my ability to see my family and having no control over what I ate and where I went humbled me.

Things I had taken for granted were gone, such as eating

what I wanted and coming and going as I pleased. The thought hit me—I could either become frustrated, keeping myself bound, or trust God. I chose the hope in God to get through this situation.

Also, ironically, I thought about how my Iraq experience indirectly prepared me for incarceration in a strange way. While in Iraq, I could not see my family or friends; I only had phone calls and letters, just like jail. Plus, I thought about past clients, former players, and friends I had encouraged when they were locked up. I got to practice what I preached myself.

One day, I began to reflect on this Bible verse often, Philippians 4:13 (KJ21): “I can do all things through Christ which strengthen me.” I thought, *Even though I am currently locked up, eventually, one day, I will come home*. Therefore, my life was not destroyed even though at times I felt that way. I embraced how God could rebuild my life. My faith was strengthened just thinking about all the times God had brought me through life’s trials. By God’s grace, I would get through this! I kept saying this to myself daily.

All these thoughts and actions were not easy to overcome. There were many distractions in jail, along with my untreated PTSD to deal with. I pushed through my depression and developed an exercise routine. I sometimes exercised with others in my cell block. Also, I wrote poems while in my cell.

I was connecting to my emotions with being in jail and coming to terms with the situation.

After my sentencing, I was eventually sent to Federal Correctional Institution (FCI) Schuykill, Pennsylvania, a medium-facility prison.

Here are some of the poems I wrote while incarcerated.

Count Time Poem

I'm inside DC CTF jail trying to free my mind, doing it during count time.

It's hard to unwind and think because everywhere I go in here I feel jinxed.

I have to keep my mind positive because I still have much to give, especially in the community where I once lived.

So I focus on God with what he is doing in my life; I'm never going to quit because his mercy and grace is making me right.

I feel like dynamite ready to explode because now the Feds are in control; I'm determined to fight improve my mind, body, and soul. Don't trip, you know God is really in control.

Hey, Feds, no matter where I'm sent, I will focus on God and turn this thing to useful time; that's how I feel during count time.

One day, I will be free and return back to the community with a more focused mind I gain doing time.

My light will shine to help mankind, especially in the "hood" where I'll be doing good.

I thirst for God's purpose in my life, so I can shine like Kid Dynamite, exploding with a bang back in the community doing the right thang!

Count time is over, and my cell door will open again. When I step out, I won't be joking; my fight is against crime that starts in your mind, but God will control your thoughts and soul once you understand *he* is in control!

—October 23, 2010, CTF

Lock Down Poem

A fight happened; some men started snapping, which led to blows, which caused a code.

COs stormed in; then they started screaming, but ready to start swinging, yelling, "Lock down, men, go to your cells."

We walked to our cell; a few people yelled. However, the command was obeyed, hoping not to get sprayed by that Mace CO used coming into the block for those fighting.

The fight was over, order was restored, but we remained in our cells upset as hell; Thinking unit locked down because some clowns got mad and threw down usually about a phone, card game, maybe over a TV show; that's how easy it is to come to blows.

Now we locked down while COs investigate the brawl, questioning the ones involved; you learned nothing gets resolved only punishment for all that's left on the block as the clock goes tick, tock.

Locked down you and your cellie talk about what happen only to change the subject so you don't start snapping.

All one can say is you must learn while locked down to pass time in a useful way; read, write, exercise, or even sleep to keep your mind at peace.

Eventually, you get out of your cell, but you realize it will happen again because life in jail is unpredictable as hell.

You'll hear the CO yell, "Lock down, step in," again. This you can bet, my friend!

—October 30, 2010, CTF

Visit Poem

You get one once a week to meet and greet; the people you love thanking God for their love.

On Marshall Block, we get face-to-face visit, no glass. Receive a hug, handshake, or kiss from the people you miss—wife, girlfriend, mother, father, son, daughter, cousin, or friend; it feels good to see them again.

You talk and get caught up on the latest; you give input on situations, give advice on life, steering them to do right, doing your best to keep everything tight.

Second, minutes go by quick, one hour, it's over; now it's their time to leave; you have to say goodbye, smiling, hugging, trying not to cry; thinking, *Damn, this hug and smile will have to hold you for a while.*

Back at my unit then to your cell wondering why Feds didn't give you bail. Oh well, you can call or write to make sure everybody is all right; then realizing where you are that's when true understanding of being a humble man begins, not having many friends.

In your mind, beginning to think of the opportunity of being free again in the community, to demonstrate your knowledge and apply yourself more so family can be proud while your actions speak loud.

Later that night, you think and pray, then go through another day in the criminal justice system maze trying not to become crazed; your mind and eyes focused on the prize to return home to family with your mind intact.

This routine can go on for months and years, causing you and your family pain and tears, but through all the madness, one thing's for sure to bring a smile to your face—that's right, visiting day, my friend.

—December 7, 2010, CTF

Another Point of View Poem

As I lay in my cell looking out my window, I see a cemetery; I wondered about those buried.

The cemetery name is Congressional. I wondered if those buried are soldiers, politicians, or just everyday citizens; were they good men, women, husbands, wives, or were they hated and despised? Did they steal, cheat, tell lies? It wouldn't be a surprise.

Did their family have grief when they died? Did they cry? Were they sad, angry, mad, or were they happy, glad, thinking about good times they had?

To my surprise, daily I see people walking, jogging, and some with their dogs throughout the graveyard; to me, it was showing no respect toward those people's lives.

I wonder why do I have this view or, if their family even knew what's going on; they probably think their loved ones are resting in peace, never expecting this disrespect, I'm only guessing.

With this view, I think about my life, family, service for this country and community, praying for immunity. Now I'm conflicted with my view causing many feelings and thoughts that race through my mind while I'm confined; not knowing how much time the judge going give my behind.

Other times, I view the cemetery feeling the realization of being locked up not being able to be in the community daily with family make me feel unmanly; I can't provide nor protect.

I'm thinking my visits seem like those who visit the dead because when they leave, I can't go with them, just like the dead. Man, this view is messing up my head.

Then I realize the hard cold facts, looking at those graves; I'm gonna die one day; how will people view my life? Some view death as the end of life or a pleasant reward to be in the presence of the Lord.

Then one morning, I awoke and realized this view is all about you, how you live and act, what you put in your mind will determine the legacy you leave behind.

Do you believe in a higher power that you trust in your darkest hour? See, jail and the graveyard are in my view now, but everlasting life, love, and forgiveness are in Jesus Christ.

—CTF Jail, July 1, 2011

CHAPTER 20

MY SENTENCING

I was in jail for ten months awaiting my sentence, which seemed like ten years to me not knowing my fate. I took a plea of guilty to three bank robberies in December 2010. I was due for sentencing, but it got rescheduled three times before I finally was sentenced in July 2011.

During this phase awaiting my sentencing, I learned about federal sentencing guidelines. My sentencing guideline was fifty-one to sixty-three months as a first-time offender and because of my age.

I used a public defender because of my guilt, not wanting to drain my family's finances for defense, especially after bonding out. I believed accepting responsibility for my actions and restoring my faith, things would work out.

One glimmer of hope that my prayers were being heard was my lawyer seemed to really have empathy and concern about my situation, unlike what you hear about public defender lawyers, not caring and working with the government to give you more time. Plus, my lawyer respected my service to the country and in the community.

I observed how my lawyer listened to me during our visit. She put together an excellent sentencing plan for me, having a social worker prepare an outstanding sentencing memorandum capturing my personal and professional experiences, which was more in depth than the government presentence report.

Plus, she obtained an independent military psychologist to evaluate how my Iraq war experiences impacted me upon my return home, affecting my impulse control and decision making and resulting in me being diagnosed with PTSD.

I received over fifty letters on my behalf to the court. The letters to the judge were about my life and service in the community before and after Iraq. Further, my lawyer argued a sentencing variance should be applied to my case because of my PTSD disability, military experiences, and no prior criminal history.

The night before sentencing, I felt at peace and hopeful. This was a feeling I hadn't felt since being in jail. I thought the months in jail reading the Bible and exercising despite circumstances strengthened my faith. Also, I was encouraged by the letters on my behalf, feeling overwhelmed with how others viewed and still believed in me. I believed God was working His will in my life and giving me strength to accept whatever time I would be given.

When I stepped into the courtroom, seeing my mother, my children, some of my friends, my coworkers, and even my army buddy Sergeant Bemore there supporting me eased some of my anxiety. I thought, to my surprise, they still believed in me! I felt blessed despite this mess I created, as strange as that may seem.

The sentencing hearing lasted like an eternity to me. My lawyer had a slide presentation that was awesome and touching. It was about my life and service in the community and Iraq. Plus, speaking on my behalf was my pastor, a community friend, and me.

The government argued for at least the minimum of

fifty-one months, stressing the danger and damage I caused in the community.

Then out of the blue, another issue came up. One county detective was there, and he whispered something to the prosecutor. The prosecutor stated there was an open warrant for my arrest for armed robbery with a weapon. It was in the presentence report too.

I began thinking back to the only time I got upset with my lawyer was when I warned her before reading the government presentence report that I had an open warrant for armed robbery. I was agitated, starting to yell at her, "I didn't commit no damn armed robbery! They lying!"

My lawyer refocused me, saying, "Don't worry about it now. Focus on this case." That was the only one she was working with me on. I remember thinking, *She got some good skills refocusing me, damn*, so I chilled out.

The federal judge who presided over my case had a reputation of giving long, harsh sentences at the federal holding jail.

During the sentencing hearing, the judge listened to everybody and noted he read my lengthy memorandum and letters to my surprise. The judge asked me to stand, and it seemed like everything was going in slow motion. He sentenced me to twenty-four months incarcerated and three years' supervised release. Further, he ordered I receive counseling.

I remember feeling nervous, standing, legs shaking. I put my hands on the table to remain steady. Then my mind was relieved with knowing how long my time was going to be. I quickly calculated in my mind that with time served in jail, I only had one year left before returning home.

Then the prosecutor argued that my custody level should be increased from low to medium facility. I wasn't worried about the custody level but became upset with being wrongly accused of an armed robbery. The judge seemed to agree with what I was thinking, questioning why this was coming up right then, especially when they knew I was detained at CTF jail Marshall Block to question or charge me.

Once back down the court cell block, I praised and thanked God for his mercy and for providing the legal team that represented me. I remember a homie was in another cell asking, "What he give you, Rob?" I told him. I remember him saying, "That's good, Rob, return back and shine." I was floored by his response because he got twenty years and now I got two years, and he wasn't mad or jealous with my short time. In retrospect, I had contact with some good men during my incarceration journey. I pray they find their way back to their families and communities.

While being transported back to jail, looking out the van window, I reflected on the bank robberies and my arrest to the present time. I had conflicting thoughts, being happy about my sentencing but frustrated with being incarcerated again.

CHAPTER 21

NO NEWS FLASH

The next day, nothing was reported in the news or newspaper about my sentencing. I became angry, thinking how the media portrayed me like Jesse James, an outlaw, in the news and newspaper upon my arrest. Further, when arrested, I was the top story on the news cycle for a day locally. There were news trucks on my street. Neighbors were asked to give thoughts about why I committed those bank robberies, and my family's home life was disrupted. I was thinking, *I get sentenced and nothing? No follow-up on my story?*

Once sentenced, I felt ashamed of how my actions had allowed society to characterize me in a negative way. I began thinking how nobody acknowledged me when I returned from Iraq. I thought, *Damn, commit a crime and I'm a hood hero and public enemy number one.*

During the sentencing hearing, life facts about me came out. However, that was not reported. Then reality hit me: the world highlights crime and negative stories. Nobody wants to hear about a veteran with PTSD and how he lost his way because of bad coping and lack of treatment. Anger boiled inside me for a month while I was awaiting transfer to federal prison. I reflected on how in the past I was portrayed in a positive manner in newspaper as a high school athlete and then as a high school head basketball coach. Now I'm a criminal, bank robber. My anger turned into motivation to write my story

Thoughts of PTSD while in Prison

I had no one clear-cut method to cope with or overcome PTSD during my incarceration. My life and war experiences didn't mean anything to other people, except the few people God had placed in my life during this journey.

To my surprise, I met other veterans and young homies who knew me as a coach, mentor, warrior citizen, and social worker in the community. They showed me respect and love. Further, I was surprised some young men still called me "Coach" or "Mr. Roberts." I was humbled and viewed it as a sign God was moving in my mess.

I remember being reluctant to talk about my feelings to anybody. Having no outlet besides exercise, I was depressed often. I learned how to hide my emotions. I thought my best option for treatment in prison was reading the Bible.

Reading God's word enhanced me spiritually, bringing hope into my life situation and future. Exercising reduced stress in a positive manner, which unleashed the frustration of my situation. Plus, I read any book I could get my hands on, enhancing my knowledge.

Participation with mental health services in prison wouldn't help me, I thought. I remember thinking being hypervigilant and agitated daily wouldn't change, considering the environment I was in. I thought in prison those feelings could benefit me.

I stayed to myself mostly, being around a small circle of homies I interacted with. I walked the track or returned to the housing unit to watch TV, mostly sports or news. I developed prison skills, stayed out of the way, kept feelings bottled up, and respected others, but if disrespected, I then struck back.

My best coping was sports, playing forty and over basketball and coaching A & B league basketball teams. I coached the DC Homie B league team to a championship. I thought if this was my last coaching job, at least I had won a championship! Matter of Time at it again!

On reflection, I can see sports have always been my refuge and a catalyst to focus on a specific task and feel good about myself.

Also, I believe my army training to recognize warning signs and dangerous situations assisted with my adjustment too. I focused on not getting more charges to prolong my sentence. Plus, I had no desire to drink or get high while in prison.

It wasn't easy coping with my freedom being lost. It was very depressing. For real, at times, I struggled, but again, my army training always kicked in, inspiring a "never quit" and "can-do" attitude.

One thing that impacted my thoughts and emotions was watching TV news and reading current news on Iraq or Afghanistan war issues. It caused me anxiety, anger, and stress. I remember feeling embarrassed, mostly about being incarcerated. I felt betrayed by society, skeptical of progress in Iraq, and stupid about not being receptive to receiving mental health services from the VA system when I was free.

While incarcerated, I remember these specific news events impacting my thoughts.

- withdrawal of military troops from Iraq
- the capture and death of Osama bin Laden

- the burning of the Koran by military troops in Afghanistan
- allegations of SSG Robert Boles murdering sixteen civilians in an Afghan village

My emotions ranged from anger to sadness to frustration about how a soldier's service is not understood or even appreciated. I wondered if my personal sacrifice was worth it and was not feeling respected professionally or socially returning from Iraq. Now I was in prison, cut off from society and struggling with my past negative actions and current thoughts. I was feeling like that Marvin Gaye song, "Trouble Man." I hoped to get through it all by continuing to march.

CHAPTER 22

FCI SCHUYKILL MADNESS

I'm sharing one experience that made my mental health feel vulnerable while at FCI Schuykill.

On Veteran's Day 2011, I became super depressed with being incarcerated and angry about my Iraq service landing me in prison. I often thought how veterans from present and previous wars were misunderstood and not provided services.

During this depressive moment, I was thinking about my family, my fellow soldiers, and the community, how I'd let them down with not being present to create positive change.

I finally requested to speak with a psychologist to assist with processing my thoughts and feelings. Part of me felt stupid asking for help; the other part wanted help.

I followed the procedure of filling out the request slip and waiting to be put on the call-out sheet to see somebody. A week later, I still was not on the call-out sheet for an appointment. After another week, I still wasn't on the call-out sheet for an appointment.

While waiting, I became more agitated and reluctantly expressed my frustration to the unit manager. He immediately took me to a psychologist on my unit but explained the staff was new. I became agitated, responding, "That's no excuse for the unprofessional response. Suppose I go off."

The unit manager said, "Well, you will go to the SHU [special housing unit], the hole, and you still won't get help, your choice."

I sucked it up and held my anger because I really wanted help. I was feeling like I was going to crash.

At the psychologist's staff office, I knocked, and the psychologist told me to come in. "What is your concern?" I remember immediately feeling no care or concern from the psychologist while being offered the opportunity to sit down. I then noticed the psychologist wasn't looking on the computer to see my record and didn't ask if I had a mental health diagnosis, which I did. *Now my damn social work skills want to kick in!* I thought.

I angrily asked why I didn't receive a response for three weeks. Then I stated, "I'm only here because the unit manager brought me."

The psychologist said, "Let's schedule an appointment, and, oh, what's your problem? Why do you want to be seen by me?"

Furious, I rose up, saying, "I'm good." I left, slamming the door, thinking, *I'm asking my oppressor, jail staff, for help.* I felt like shit and was angered about asking for help.

The unit manager stepped out into hallway and told me to cool off, go to my cell, and not cause any problems because he would send me to the "hole." I left, not responding. I returned to my cell, feeling like a fool for asking for help! I realized prison is a tough environment to receive mental health help in. I was embarrassed that my feelings and emotions caused me to feel inadequate at that point in my life. I remember thinking, *My old ass going to do five hundred push-ups tomorrow to feel better.*

After two days fighting negative urges to act out my anger, I became more depressed while trying to suppress these thoughts. I started to feel helpless at controlling my emotions and thoughts.

The next day, feeling like I was going to explode, I talked with one of my homies. During my discussion about what happened with the unit psychologist, my homie said, "These people up here getting paid doing nothing." That spurred me to follow up on this lack of service.

The next day, I decided to speak up. Now at Schuykill FCI, the warden and staff were at the dining hall on the walkway to be available to inmates. I took a deep breath and walked over to the warden, showing my request slip for psychologist services. I expressed my complaints of lack of response. The warden listened to me and sent me to see the psychologist department supervisor further down the line, pointing at me and saying, "See this inmate."

I walked down the line to see the supervisor. The supervisor looked at my request slip and listened to me. The response was an excuse to me that the staff was new, but I should have stated specifically what my problem was on the request slip. I answered, "I couldn't write my concern, but I requested to be seen and that should be enough to be seen." Then, there we went with the questions that always angered me and made me skeptical of receiving help. "Are you taking medication? Do you feel like harming yourself or others?"

I realized at that moment I was in "prison." The reality is it's punishment for your crime. Also, safety is the number one concern for staff, not treatment, although doctors and mental health staff are available.

Later that day, I was walking the track. I began thinking I should not look for a human answer. I understood there was no concerned committed treatment in a prison setting; therefore, it forced me to turn to God even more. I turned more to spiritual readings and having faith in God.

Also, while at FCI Schuykill, I began to reflect on my transition from Iraq and prayed to respond to the lack of empathy, concern, and procedural rules in prison better than I did in the community. Plus, I thought about how not to fall into the "Why me?" trap again. In my mind, I began to deal with my reality (being locked up) in a positive manner, especially with not facing a long sentence.

On reflection, I'd learned that in prison and at the VA hospital, there were going to be roadblocks that one had to learn to overcome. I thought I could if I stayed connected to and in tune with God's word daily.

While working out daily to get in shape to feel good about myself and reading the Bible, I honestly looked at my character defects, remembering my twelve steps.

As I got close to my release date, my anxiety again was building regarding my return to the community. I wondered if I would get another job. Could I be a good role model to my children and grandchildren again? Would I make a positive adjustment, returning to live with my mother while being sensitive and responsive to her advancing age and medical needs? How would I process everything upon my release?

Then I just thought, *Believe in Bible verse Psalm 142:7: "Bring my soul out of prison, that I may praise thy name: the righteous shall compass me about; for thou shalt deal bountifully with me."*

I read this Bible verse daily, having hope. A week before my release, I remember thinking eventually how God's word would manifest in my life. Well, I'd find out in a "matter of time." Once released, I was praying for strength and grace.

CHAPTER 23

TRANSITION

Everybody will experience transition in his or her life—in school, jobs, relationships, and so on. How you respond during transition impacts you mentally and emotionally. I experienced transitions as a military veteran and "returning citizen," a term for a person released from jail or prison.

My transition from Iraq deployment back to the civilian world was difficult. All the necessary behaviors needed in a combat zone were not healthy or acceptable in society. For instance, hypervigilance—while on a convoy stuck in traffic, you could drive upstream, in the opposite direction, to keep going or ram a car out of the way. In the civilian world, you'd go to jail or get a traffic ticket.

My transition from prison was similar to the Iraq transition. I was hypervigilant and agitated often. However, I thought my spirituality was improving, giving me faith that I would have future success.

The following are thoughts and comparisons of a veteran and returning citizen.

- Military veteran—society acknowledges you and deems your service respectable action for the country. You can receive parades and welcome-home programs.
- Returning citizen—society views you as a lawbreaker. Your family and community, you hope, accepts you back. I believe my black and brown community respects returning citizens more than veterans, because it seems more common.

In both situations, war veteran and returning citizen, people experience relationship issues and personal, family, job, and housing difficulties.

Also, I feel how one perceives knowledge and belief can enhance or disrupt one's transition back to the community.

Knowledge is what you experience and learn; you see results.

Belief is what you want to happen and you think will happen with certain action.

I received conflicting messages from the world as both. As a military veteran, it was "Why you fight the white man's war? But thanks for your service." As a returning citizen, it was "What made you rob a bank. Glad you home," but I was restricted in resuming my professional career because of the felony.

One thing sticks out in comparing the two transitions: how others receive you matters, so respect both journeys and provide supportive services and treatment to enhance the transition home for both.

CHAPTER 24

RELEASED FROM PRISON

My release date from Schuykill, June 5, 2012, was a bittersweet day. I had completed my federal prison time, and my three years' supervised release was next.

However, I knew that warrant in Maryland was next too. Homies were split about whether Maryland would be waiting outside the gates. Some thought I would go home and then have to turn myself in, or I would be arrested when I reported to the supervised release officer. I was getting stressed again! I remember having that frustrated feeling like when outprocessing from Iraq. I silently prayed for help with all these thoughts.

I was processing out of prison, and you guessed it, going through the door, I was placed under arrest, charged, and held in Schuykill County Jail, waiting for Maryland County to pick me up.

I was held in custody for fourteen days, waiting for Maryland County's slow ass. I spent the time in "the hole" because I had a problem with processing into the jail.

The problem arose with having to take off my Timberland work boots I'd brought and was allowed to wear while in Feds. They were putting me in flip-flops, no tennis shoes or Jackie Chan slip-ons, which I refused to wear. The captain of the jail shift came to where I was at and saw me refusing to go to a unit. He said, "You're a visitor, not going be held here long, so just cooperate." I still bucked until those two big football lineman correctional officers came in, and then I braced for the ass whooping. The captain looked at me and said, "Well, how about going to the hole, which will solve everybody's problem, and you will be wearing those flip-flops to the hole." The silver lining was they let me take all my reading materials and the Bible I had from the Feds—and I avoided an ass whooping. I felt God had answered my prayer by leading me through this journey again.

The Maryland sheriffs finally picked me up and transported me to county jail. Once there, I began dealing with these bogus charges. I was looking at thirty years with all the charges I had from allegedly committing two armed robberies. Again, I didn't do this! So, I decided I'd ride it out in county jail, go to trial with a public defender, and get found not guilty. In the back of my mind, I was thinking, *No way I'll be found guilty, but what if? That's a lot of time, damn.*

I was detained in county jail for a month before something strange happened. One day, I was told I had a legal visit. At a meeting with who I thought was my lawyer, I was told, "Just plead guilty. Cop out to five years, do three years, and go home." I banged on the door, saying, "My visit's over. Let me go back to my unit." I immediately called my older daughter and told her I needed a paid lawyer and to get me bailed out to deal with this. I was blessed my family had the resources to do this because it seemed like I was going be railroaded to prison. Once released on bond in August, I prepared for my trial with my lawyer.

My trial was in November. It lasted one day. My lawyer team represented me well and showed how bogus these charges against me were. The jury deliberated two hours, and I was found not guilty. I remember walking out of court, just taking a deep breath, and saying, "Now on to the supervised release journey."

My supervision was transferred from Maryland to the DC Federal office. I successfully completed my three-year supervised release. Continue to March!

CHAPTER 25

RECEPTIVE TO TREATMENT, SECOND TRANSITION HOME

Returning home from prison, I was receptive to mental health treatment. I was not reluctant like I had been returning from Iraq.

Going back to the vet center, I noticed how many Vietnam vets were going to group, and I was in groups with them. Before, in my first transition from Iraq, I felt we had nothing in common, different ages and different wars.

Now participating in groups with Vietnam vets, I appreciated their wisdom and inspiration. Most had been drafted; the last war had been heavy frontline fighting, taking hills, and so on, and they returned home to a society that viewed war as being useless, bad. TV images of war shocked America. Thus, they were called "baby killers." They came home without impactful help, without resources, and with a lack of mental health support. Now these men returned and continued to train by going to groups to retrain their minds. I thought, *If they can do it, I damn well can too.*

Also, I thought the Vietnam vets' participation was the best model to see firsthand that you can teach an old dog new tricks. I again thought, *I can do this too. Roof!*

While being receptive to treatment, I noticed Desert Storm, Iraq, and Afghanistan soldiers shared a close bond with more common battlefield experiences. Plus, it seemed all soldiers struggled with issues, not just me. I felt comfortable around my era of soldiers naturally. At first, I really embraced going to groups at the vet center. Then I became open to going to the VA hospital and participating in an anger management class, PTSD groups, and relationship group.

Also, during this transition, I was able to see all the men in the groups had common issues—PTSD, alcohol, drugs, divorce, and anger management issues to name a few. Therefore, I felt connected and hopeful while participating in these groups.

Vet 2 Vet Poem

We can talk that talk, feel that soldier life walk.

Anger, alcohol, drugs, divorce, and jail all these issues we might share; if we listen to one another, we can learn not to repeat mistakes.

Feel good talking to my brothers and sisters in arms because you don't get alarmed with cussing and yelling; there is no overcorrecting with language like the civilians.

Keep it up, get that stress off your chest, keep coming to group you be reminded you're around America's best, who learn how to adapt and overcome.

We were taught buddy aid in all branches of service, so let's help each other out in group; show the world we have no fear while moving on up out from this PTSD mental angry, depressed swirl.

Let's continue to March; we can all heal, restore our life to be the real deal!

—In community, February 2014

CHAPTER 26

CHANGE

We cannot change a person, nor can we force a change in values or attitudes. We can force behavior for a period of time, but as soon as the controls are removed, the person will revert to what he or she feels comfortable doing. We can only motivate, encourage, and provide the opportunity for change to occur and then hope the person will choose to change. This was on a handout I read while incarcerated.

While incarcerated, I often thought about change. I didn't like where I was at. I was upset with my actions that had gotten me incarcerated, and I was hurt with the pain from the difficulties that my actions had brought to my family. Wow, my return from Iraq, my experiences over there, and how I was received by work, family, and friends changed my values and attitudes.

Use of alcohol altered my feelings and judgment, which led me to become unlawful. The things I mentioned caused me to change from how I acted before going to Iraq.

My time being incarcerated motivated me to change back to the old but new and improved Damon—a God-fearing, respectful, law-abiding, humble, community-conscious man. I realized nobody could feel my pain, hurt, despair, anger, and resentment but God. Through God's grace and wisdom and me applying godly principles in my life, I could endure, recover, and return back to society a changed man. Also, I had faith and trust God would put people and opportunities in place to assist me. I aspired to be a catalyst for change, to have a positive attitude, while being humble and open to change.

"Men are anxious to improve their circumstances but are unwilling to improve themselves; they therefore remain bound," James Allen wrote in *As a Man Thinketh.*

This quote just magnifies that making positive change in your life requires work and effort. I have experienced the success of hard work before in achieving my goals and accomplishments in my personal, professional, and military careers.

I'm determined now to have a better transition from prison than I did from Iraq. I realize change starts with my thoughts—no self-pity or blaming others—and have learned how to positively release anger so it doesn't turn to resentment, which cripples self-growth and willingness to change. In other words, *no "Why me?" syndrome.*

I learned a something while in jail that is simply stated but really sparked a change in my mind. The saying is "There are three types of people—one, those who make things happen; two, those who watch things happen; and three, those who wonder how things happen." My goal is to be the type of person who causes change by making positive things happen in my midst.

Another saying is "There are three types of mind-sets of people: great minds discuss ideas, mediocre minds discuss things, and small minds discuss people." I want to challenge myself with being a person of change who discusses ideas that create positive actions, plans, and support to veterans, ex-offenders, and our community.

For a veteran, the ability to cope with hidden battlefield injuries, PTSD, traumatic brain injury (TBI), or physical wounds relates to how an individual responds mentally and physically to change. A person has to be willing to retrain, relearn, and rethink to overcome changes in his or her life—no self-pity or blaming others. One has to learn how to release anger, so it doesn't turn to resentment, which cripples self-growth and the willingness to change.

Also, veterans and returning citizens have to draw upon past experiences where they had previous success and apply the lessons through productive, law-abiding actions.

I reflected on my experience as a social worker, warrior citizen, and returning citizen, and I believe in the concept of providing instruction and assistance, to others. People deserve a second chance. Also, one should learn how to apply the golden rule, treating others like you would like to be treated. I believe this concept is important in working with people during their transition back into the community.

I realize not being able to express my feelings, pain, concerns, and problems during transition home caused me more problems. The hypocrisy of Iraqi Freedom made me cynical of life and religious views; therefore, I changed. Things I valued, such as coaching, I lost upon my return home. This crushed me internally, changing my mind-set about my professional life.

While incarcerated though, I *changed*, slowly regaining my faith and trust and renewing my relationship with God. Through my various readings—historical and educational—and watching national and world news, I gained perspective. Through participation in Bible study groups, I gained insight and inspiration with a new direction of being a positive producer of change in my community.

I now view my past military, social work, high school

basketball coach, mentor, drill instructor, and classroom instructor career as being a seed planter for positive change.

Now I'm determined to be a catalyst of change in my community, being a positive seed planter. I want to help plant seeds of positive change in the community for military veterans and ex-offenders.

CHAPTER 27

MOVING ON TO THE FUTURE

Writing this book, I relived the joy and pain of my life experiences—my feelings upon transitioning from Iraq, thoughts concerning treatment, feelings about being incarcerated, and my experiences transitioning from prison.

I learned a lot during my treatment journey, participating in different models, such as present- and past-focused treatment, co-occurring PTSD and substance or alcohol abuse, and the AA Twelve-Step Program.

I pray this book gives an example of how PTSD and alcohol abuse impact a person. Also, I hope it encourages other veterans and returning citizens to consider the importance of mental health treatment.

Further, I pray it inspires service providers to create new programs to enhance transition services for veterans and returning citizens.

Thank you for letting me share! God bless!

PHOTO GALLERY

REDSKINS

MATTER OF TIME

BOYS & GIRLS CLUB